Robert B. Roosevelt

Five Acres too Much

a truthful elucidation of the attractions of the country, and a careful consideration

of the question of profit and loss as involved in amateur farming

Robert B. Roosevelt

Five Acres too Much

a truthful elucidation of the attractions of the country, and a careful consideration of the question of profit and loss as involved in amateur farming

ISBN/EAN: 9783337230517

Printed in Europe, USA, Canada, Australia, Japan

Cover: Foto ©Lupo / pixelio.de

More available books at **www.hansebooks.com**

FIVE ACRES TOO MUCH.

A TRUTHFUL ELUCIDATION

OF

The Attractions of the Country,

AND

A CAREFUL CONSIDERATION OF THE

Question of Profit and Loss as involved in
Amateur Farming,

WITH MUCH

VALUABLE ADVICE AND INSTRUCTION TO THOSE ABOUT
PURCHASING LARGE OR SMALL PLACES
IN THE RURAL DISTRICTS.

NEW AND ENLARGED EDITION.

BY

ROBERT BARNWELL ROOSEVELT,

AUTHOR OF "GAME FISH OF NORTH AMERICA," "SUPERIOR FISHING,"
"FLORIDA AND THE GAME WATER BIRDS," "PROGRESSIVE PETTICOATS,"
"FISH HATCHING AND FISH CATCHING," ETC.

NEW YORK:
O. JUDD CO. DAVID W. JUDD, Pres.
751 Broadway.
1885.

TO
THE WRITERS OF BOOKS
ON
FARMING, GARDENING, HORTICULTURE, AGRICULTURE, AND FLORICULTURE,

THIS WORK IS RESPECTFULLY DEDICATED,

AS AN EVIDENCE
OF WHAT CAN BE DONE AND WHAT WONDERFUL RESULTS
CAN BE PRODUCED BY A CAREFUL STUDY OF
THEIR DIRECTIONS AND STRICT OBE-
DIENCE TO THEIR RULES;

AND

AS A SLIGHT TESTIMONIAL TO THE ACCURACY, LUCIDITY,
AND PRACTICABILITY OF THE ADVICE WHICH THEY
GIVE AND THE EXPERIENCES THEY DESCRIBE;

IN THE SINCERE HOPE
THAT THEY WILL NEVER WEARY OF COMPOSING BOOKS
EQUALLY TRUTHFUL, TRUSTWORTHY,
AND INTERESTING.

THE AUTHOR.

CONTENTS.

INTRODUCTION.

Apotheosis of the Country, especially of such Portions of the Country as the Author has for sale.—Many Attractions and still more Lots at Flushing.—Simplicity of Farming, and Lucidity of Agricultural Books.—Profits and Pleasures of Rural Life.......Page ix

CHAPTER I.
A COW.

Special Points about the Bovine Race.—Directions in Feeding.—Preparations to receive the Animal.—Her Arrival.—An awful Pause.—The Fray about to begin.—Intelligence of Cows and Biddies.—Victory.—A Calm.—Cow Complainings.—Approaching Storm.—A Tempest in a back Yard.—Soothing Effects of "Mash."—Immense Profits and glorious Prospects for the Future.—Peculiarities and Eccentricities of the Race as exhibited in a confined Space.—She is sent to the Country for the benefit of her Health.. 19

CHAPTER II.
A HOUSE, PLANS, AND SPECIFICATIONS.

Wonderful architectural Genius of the Author.—He admires himself and consults his Friends.—Difficulties in obtaining "just the Thing."—Want of Time.—Free Trade in Houses advocated as superior to Home Production.—The imported Article falls into the Hands of a Philistine named Barney.—A fresh Arrival.—The House comes, but the Builder does not.—The Charge of the Light Brigade, and Flight of the Housekeeper.................. 37

CHAPTER III.
MORE LIVE-STOCK—A HORSE AND A PIG. WHICH IS THE NOBLER ANIMAL?

Beauties of the Pig.—Defects of the Horse.—The dearest Pig and the dearest Horse, each in their way.—A haunted House, and the

Effect of Ghosts on Horses.—The Ghost Story precisely as it occurred.—Are Ghosts liable to Damages when they frighten Horses into fits of running away?—Equine Eccentricities.—Practical Playfulness..Page 61

CHAPTER IV.
THE COUNTRY, AND HOW TO GET THERE.

Easy Accessibility of Flushing.—An improving Railroad.—Education by Steam.—True Principles of Travel........................ 77

CHAPTER V.
A WELL.

A Well, considered classically and otherwise.—A Cat in search of the Truth.—A Catastrophe.—Pumps and Vanities of Life.—A poor Sucker.—Hydraulic Pressure.................................... 86

CHAPTER VI.
A KITCHEN GARDEN.

Advantages thereof.—Things to have.—You wish you may get them.—Ornamental as opposed to practical Views.—A dissolving View.—Bad Beginnings do not always make a good Ending.—Daniel O'Rourke's as a grazing Crop.—The new-mown Hay.—Its Flavor and Flower.—Remarkable Results of Gardening for Profit...... 97

CHAPTER VII.
THE FLOWER GARDEN.

Architectural Skill set at defiance by practical Difficulties.—Result of too much Greenness.—A Disappointment....................... 111

CHAPTER VIII.
POULTRY.

Strange Attack of Somnolency.—Dogs and Peppers as awakeners.—The right Thing in the wrong Place.—A Hen lays herself out.—Twenty pair of Chickens raise the Hair of one Mink........ 124

CHAPTER IX.
FALL WORK.

A Fortune in Strawberries.—How to get it out.—Debility developed.—Science to the Rescue.—The wonderful Effects of a Liquid Fertilizer. — No Farmer should fail to have such a Thing in the House..Page 136

CHAPTER X.
PROFIT AND LOSS.

Immense pecuniary Advantages of high old Farming.—Exactitude the Foundation of Success in Life.—A plain Statement.—General Reflections.—An amateur Butcher.—Boiled salt Pork.......... 148

CHAPTER XI.
THE FLUSHING SKATING-POND—A DIGRESSION.

A nice Man as an Ice-man... 161

CHAPTER XII.
THE SECOND YEAR.

A new Start, with no Drawbacks.—Immense Results, but not precisely what was wanted.—The great Pea turns out small.—Wonderful obstinacy of Plants... 169

CHAPTER XIII.
SCIENCE.

Knowledge is Power.—The new Flower.—A Thing of Beauty.—Appearance contrasted with Perfume.—The Fox is the Finder.. 179

CHAPTER XIV.
A SECOND DIGRESSION—FAIRY TALES FOR LITTLE FOLKS.

Retributive Justice.—Don't be such a Goose...................... 189

CHAPTER XV.
NUISANCES, INHUMAN AND HUMAN. PETS—THE CHARM OF COUNTRY LIFE.

With a few Reservations.—Flies on the Rampage.—Wonderful Discovery.—Dogs on Seedlings.—A Hop-toad Hunt............... 203

CHAPTER XVI.
BUTTER-MAKING. SEEDS AND THE DEVIL.

Butter-making in all its Attractions.—The Cream unequal to the Emergency.—Some Things can't be Done as well as Others.—Electrical Phenomena.—Gathering Seed.—Incidental Reference to Satan and his Works—not his agricultural ones............. 216

CONTENTS.

CHAPTER XVII.
SUCCESS OF THE YEAR.

A second Year's Balance-sheet.—Still greater Promises.—Success assured.—Every Man should be his own Market Gardener.—No dearth of Onions.—Transported at the Result.—The last of the family Horse.—He closes his Career by a wonderful Feat in drawing Teeth..Page 233

CHAPTER XVIII.
PREPARATIONS FOR REMOVAL.

The window Garden.—Warm Work.—Immense Resources of Science.—Mind against Matter.—What can the Matter be?—The new Flower 253

CHAPTER XIX.
A GREAT RUNNER.

A perfect Jonah.—Very fine, only don't do it again.—A Gourd runs away with its Master.—A changeable Crimson.—A new Specimen of Flax, Red one Year and Yellow the next......... 266

CHAPTER XX.
A BEAUTIFUL NEW COACH.

A Rockaway stricken with Palsy.—Sudden Recovery.—Honesty of country Mechanics their best Recommendation.—A Roof over one's Head.—Its Necessity, as well as Beauty.—A Fellow-feeling makes us willing to lend Shingles.—The latter End............ 283

CHAPTER XXI.
THREE HUNDRED ACRES NOT ENOUGH.

New Farms.—More Land.—No Rooms for Mushrooms.—Many Sects of Insects.—The Squash.—Unexpected Fungi.—The Triumph that Grazed Defeat.—The Joys of Memory....297

INTRODUCTION.

IT was in consequence of reading a little volume called "Ten Acres Enough"—a practical and statistical, as well as, in certain points, a poetical production—that I came to prepare this volume. In that work a charming and interesting account is given of the successful attempt of a Philadelphia mechanic to redeem a strip of exhausted land of ten acres in extent. In the course of it, a vast deal of advice and most valuable directions are given on the subject of planting and sowing, draining and reaping, manuring and pruning; berries and fruits, vines and vegetables, are duly considered; and the question of outlay and income, expenses and receipts, losses and profits, is forever ding-donged into one's ears. So useful is the instruction it contains, that no one should think of buying a farm, experimenting in rural life, or even reading this book, without first perusing that one. To be sure, the author forgets occasionally some minor matters—such as clothing, food, and the like, leaving his family naked and unfed for several years—but that is doubtless due to his poetical temperament and intense love of nature. In the same spirit, therefore, no matter how frequently I may refer to money matters in the course of the following pages, even if I should occasionally condescend to speak of food and raiment—those commonplace necessities—it must be understood to be with no sordid view; and if I keep these matters before the reader's attention, it will be for the sole purpose of benefiting and enlightening him, and pointing out clearly the financial consequence of investing in rural residences.

The country—how beautiful it is! To a man wearied with the cares of city life; who has pursued an exhausting profession for several years with vigorous energy; who has taken a hand in politics, attended caucuses and Conventions, and helped to "run the machine;" who has a philanthropic turn of mind, and gone on committees and made public collections; and who, moreover, has abundant means—this, though last, is by no means least—the country, with its green leaves, its lovely flowers, its waving grass, its early vegetables, and its luscious fruits, is most attractive; and where a residence can be obtained which combines all these luxuries with pure air, and no chills and fever, and which is not too remote from city life and its attractions, it is as near to Paradise as this world permits.

There are many such places near New York. Gorgeous villas dot the banks of the Hudson, and congregate together thickly on Staten Island; there are beautiful spots along the coves of Westchester County, and persons who do not mind expatriating themselves go to Jersey; but there is one locality that far surpasses all others. The steep banks of the Hudson, cut off as they are from the westerly winds by the Palisades and higher hills beyond them, are uncomfortably hot; Staten Island is overrun by sour-krout-eating, lager-beer-drinking, and small-bird-shooting Germans, who trespass with Teutonic determination wherever their notions of sportsmanship or the influence of lager leads them; Westchester County, like some of our famous *prima donnas*, is fair to look upon, but great on shakes—too much so for perfect repose; and Jersey will be a pleasant place to live in when the inhabitants, individually and as a government, cease to live off strangers.

The locality referred to—the chosen spot of this earth—the Eden of a country village—has none of these drawbacks. An invigorating breeze blows over pure salt marshes; Germans do not trespass nor make one afraid; no man residing there has ever had a case of chills and fever, no matter what may have happened to his neighbor, where the boys are forever out o' nights and exposed to the dew; and the inhabitants are always ready to kindly take a stranger in.

It is a village, and yet country houses stand embosomed in majestic trees; cows pasture in the vacant lots and bellow in the streets; nurseries for the propagation of trees and shrubs give a condensed edition of miniature forests, and furnish in one rod the flowers that Nature, if left alone to her parsimonious way, would scatter over an acre; gas is in the residences, pigs root in the public roads, and early peas are combined with plank side-walks. This unequaled concentration of attractions can be reached in thirty minutes from either the upper or lower part of the city—of course New York city is meant, as no one need leave Philadelphia or Boston to get into the country—and by a most delightful route, partly on water and partly by railroad. The trains run every hour all through the day, and the line is the safest in the world. This spot, so desirable, so infinitely superior to all others, is Flushing, Long Island.

I have some property at Flushing which I should

like to sell in lots to suit purchasers; in fact, it is five acres of such lots—the five acres that this book is all about. I owned this superior investment when "Ten Acres Enough" led me to thinking that if the author could make such a delicious thing of a plot of sand in New Jersey, as much could probably be done with half the area in the fine soil of Flushing. Unfortunately, my land had no improvements, but then it was a magnificent level square, precisely like a block in the city, and admirably adapted to building. Otherwise my five acres were full as good as the half of his ten acres; the grass seemed to be abundant, for the cows of the entire neighborhood had grazed on it from time immemorial; a previous owner had been once known to plant cabbages, and the tradition is that they grew and came out cabbages, and did not, as they usually do, spread themselves and become very fine but rather loose leaves. The soil was deep, a well having been sunk on the adjoining property without descending beyond it, or reaching any water worth speaking of; and the exposure was as sunny as could be desired—there being only six trees, and one of those in doubtful health, on the entire five acres. Teachers generally say, on receiving a new pupil from another master, that there is more trouble to unlearn than to learn; here there was nothing to be undone—everything was to be done. It was not exactly a virgin soil, but, like a lovely widow, it had lain fallow—a friendly farmer made use of that word—so long, that it would be grateful for the touch of a rake or a hoe. There was no garden, no fence, no orchard, and no fruit-trees of any kind except one apple-tree, but then the nurseries and a little labor would make this right.

An unpleasant suspicion crossed my mind that perhaps it would have been better if some of these things had been done to my hand, and that possibly I was not exactly the man to do them in the best way; but a second perusal of "Ten Acres Enough" was enough for me, and these absurd doubts were banished forever. If an uneducated mechanic could leave Philadelphia, rescue a decaying farm, and make it splendidly remunerative, why could not an educated lawyer from New York convert an uninjured farm into the eighth or ninth—we Americans have added a few to them—wonder of the world?

The affair was as simple as could be. With a class-book of botany, a recipe from Professor Mapes, a few cuttings of some wonderful new berry—of which, doubtless, there were plenty, and Bridgman's "Gardener's Assistant," the result was certain. It was merely a question of seeds, weeds, and manure—the first and last to be encouraged, and the other to be eradicated.

After all, what is the wonderful science in farming? You put a seed in the ground, and it comes up—that is, if it does come up—either a pea or a bean, a carrot or a turnip, and, with your best skill and greatest learning, you can not plant a pea and induce it to come up a bean, or convert a carrot into a turnip. As for planting, any fool can do that, and as for making it grow, the wisest man in the land can not effect it. These and a few other similar arguments were entirely conclusive, and soon visions of the accomplished fact engrossed my mind.

I should have a neat, modest, small, but cosy little house; square, for economy's sake, but surrounded on all sides by a deep piazza; the garden should be filled with delicious vegetables, fruits, and berries, the earliest and best of their kinds; there should be a magnificent bed of asparagus—that king of the kitchen garden—a dozen long rows of strawberries, with fruit as luscious as a young girl's lips; Bartlett pears, early peas, peaches and cream—the latter only indirectly vegetable—cauliflowers, tomatoes, mushrooms, lettuce—every thing, in fact, that a gentleman eats when he can get it, and nothing that he eschews when he can do no better. The residue of the farm was to be partly orchard and partly market garden, and this was to supply the family during the winter and pay the expenses of the household.

It is an immense satisfaction, of a hot evening in summer, even in the prematurely scorching days of June, to leave the city, after a long day of labor and trouble, and, rushing away with railroad speed into the country, to enjoy the delicious air and cool breeze, to sit beneath the outspreading trees, to wander through the woods, to bathe in the brook, to doze or smoke in the shade. The scent of the blossoms or the hay, or no smell at all, is such an exquisite relief from the customary odors of New York streets. The sun seems to lose half and the air to gain double its ordinary power. The pleasures are so innocent, the matters of interest so pure, the mind is braced but not wearied. The garden, whether kitchen or flower garden—those delightful adjuncts of a country place—is such an infinite source of health, improvement, and delight. Man, confined to the city by dire necessity of money-making, recognizing the country as the natural sphere of his existence, dreams of a neat, quiet, retired country place, and books such as "Ten Acres Enough" persuade him to convert these dreams into realities.

I had always been troubled with similar visions,

although by a strange fatality my education in country matters had been wofully neglected, for I could hardly distinguish tomato-vines from egg-plants, and had not the remotest notion of modes or seasons of planting; but, now that there was a possibility that these imaginings might be realized, I was so charmed, that I resolved to record my experiences for the guidance and instruction of others. Thus it came about that this work was written; and if it is occasionally defective in style and irregular in plan, it is probably not more so than was my farming.

In looking over this introduction with a view to getting up a revised and enlarged edition of "Five Acres too Much" some fifteen years after the original was written, I find little to add and less to change in it. Finding my farm of five acres so remarkably improving, productive, and remunerative, I purchased one of twenty-five, afterwards another of a hundred and twenty, and now I own, have, hold, possess, till, and enjoy three hundred and fifty broad acres of health and fertility. To-day I am the "past grand" of farmers, for I have raised the giant squash which admits to the innermost circles of the initiated. My readers will be glad to learn that Patrick is still with me. My farming and my writings on farm-life would have been a failure without his efficient aid, and he still possesses that versatility of resources which in the original pages of this work almost elevated him to the rank of genius. I have added some of our modern experiences, and believe the patient reader will find them fully equal to anything I had previously chronicled. When my dear old friend and instructor Mr. Horace Greeley first read my humble contribution to the literature of plough and spade, he pronounced the unpleasant criticism that "the man who wrote that book ought to be kicked." But I felt that he was in error, or that possibly jealousy rather than public spirit dictated his cynical words, because "What I knew about Farming" differed in some essentials from what he knew, although we had in the main reached the same results. An additional chapter gives my subsequent operations, which were as gloriously successful as the previous ones, and prove beyond dispute the delight, benefit, and profit of rural occupations when they are intelligently conducted by a citizen of liberal education, scientific attainments, and vigorous back.

THE AUTHOR.

May, 1885.

FIVE ACRES TOO MUCH.

CHAPTER I.

A COW.

IT was early in winter when I made up my mind finally to erect a country house on the Flushing five acres. Plans, and size, and arrangements were in the vague and misty future; for months the ground could not be broken to build the foundations, and little could be done besides preparing for the next year. The first thing that seemed of vital importance was the stock. Pigs and chickens could be obtained at any time; horses had to be had, of course, but need not bother one till the last moment; but a cow was a creature that must be taken when a good one offered. Moreover, I have a weakness for cows: it is a purely theoretical interest, for my knowledge is less than moderate, not even extending to the mode of milking them; but their big eyes, and gentle manners, and unnecessary horns, and split feet, have always filled my heart with love and wonder. Horses are miserable creatures, invariably doing precisely what they ought not to do, kicking when they ought to go, going when they ought to stand still, balking when their owner is in the most frantic haste; forever sick, or lame, or requiring to be shod—a pest, a nuisance, and a bore. But cows do not balk, or run, or go lame, or need shoeing; and although they occasionally kick over the milk-pail, it is probably with good reason or with the best of intentions. They have nice long coats that keep them from catching cold in winter, and have an odd way of perspiring through their noses that is as curious as it is interesting. A cow is a model—without referring to this last peculiarity—for a wife; she is gentle, good, and beautiful, and never makes a fuss. The first point, therefore, was to buy a cow.

I had a friend living at Flushing named Augustus Weeville, who had been there several years, and who had acquired great knowledge of the intricacies of rural performances, and, among other things, was learned in cows. In fact, he was learned in most farming matters, and, being naturally proud of his adopted village, and interested in my success in emigrating thither, gave me throughout his valuable advice and assistance.

Of course, his aid was called in on the cow question, and equally, of course, he knew an Irishman—by-the-by, what can be the reason that Irishmen are the only people that have cows to sell? Is it because they love cows, or hate them? The whole world knows their "strong weakness" for pigs, but do they collect rare specimens of cows out of pure affection, to dispose of to curiosity-seekers having good homes? Or is it that they love pigs too well to endure the presence of a rival, and dispose of the bovine race as fast as they obtain them? However that may be, if you ever want a cow, an Irishman will want to sell you one; and this particular Irishman had a particularly fine animal—just the thing for the occasion.

Before purchasing, I made a few elementary inquiries—as to what cows eat, how much exercise they needed, in what manner they were to be stabled, and how many quarts of oats they would require daily. My friend replied that they preferred a warm mash, to be given three times a day; and when he saw from my countenance that my mind was a blank on the subject of warm mashes, he explained that hot water was poured upon bran and meal mixed, and that the mixture was then usually called a mash, although why and wherefore he could not distinctly say. Then, carried away by the extent of his knowledge, and rousing to the subject, he went into the habits of cows in general; that he thought ship-stuff was an excellent change of diet; that they liked hay, turnips, carrots, potato-peelings, bread, slops of all kinds that were not greasy; that they were not fed oats, and required no exercise and no care in the stable, but stood in the sun all day long, winking and blinking with contentment, and put themselves to bed at night; that the one he referred to was not young, but gentle and a good milker; and mentioned incidentally that he hardly knew where I would keep her in the city, as no cow would ever go down the area steps and through a narrow hall-way into a back yard.

Now I knew nothing of bran, and meal, and ship-stuff, and only listened with an attempt at an intelligent smile, satisfied that the articles could be purchased by name, and without explaining their nature; but I was well aware that the yard was the only place in which to keep the cow, and that the road to it was down the steps and through the lower hall; at least, if there was any other way thither, I had not yet discovered it, and I had owned my house then some twenty years. So this casual objection was quite a serious one, and we were compelled to discuss the feasibility of leading the animal up the front steps—a proceeding, however, which would have required her to go down the back ones—or hoisting her over the fence. As these measures did not seem practicable, and a cow must be had, my friend mildly suggested that several Irishmen with a stout rope might drag her through the passage-way; and as my faith in the nature of cows was illimitable, it was determined to make the purchase on the chance. The weight of a cow was to me an utterly unknown quantity, and the floor she was to pass over having once, on a previous occasion, and without any great strain, given way, a carpenter had to be called in to strengthen it. He, in his enthusiasm, and being probably as ignorant as myself, used so many supports that it would have been strong enough to carry an elephant, while four able-bodied men were engaged from a neighboring stable, and provided with a good-sized rope, so that we were fully prepared for any emergency.

In order that there may be no mistake in the debit and credit of this transaction, it must be known that the cow cost $100, to be delivered at the door free of charge. So this sum must be charged to principal as so much invested in stock, whether it ever entered my back yard or not; and the interest on it will hereafter be one of the current expenses, amounting, at seven per cent., to exactly $7 a year. It is essential that these matters should be watched; "look after the pennies, and the pounds will take care of themselves;" and the point would be whether the cow's milk and so forth would hereafter pay $7 annually net profit.

The day appointed to receive my new pet arrived, and with it the animal, while four brawny, red-handed Irishmen, strong enough to pick her up and carry her if she resisted, were at the door. They at once became excited, and prepared for action, and the cow looked wild and threatening as they closed in around her. Her owner, who was leading her with a cord, called out "soo-so-o-o" in a deprecatory manner, that evidently produced no effect; he, however, got her head to the first step, where she hesitated, and began to sniff suspiciously. The moment of action had evidently come, and I was about to shout to my supporters, who had been carefully instructed as to their duties, "Up, guards, and at her," when the lower door opened, and an intelligent Irish female appeared, holding a turnip in her hand. The effect was magical; the creature's countenance changed instantly; turnips evidently had been scarce with her, or her owner, not thinking it worth while to waste food that would not be paid for, had left her hungry; she advanced her nose expectantly, and, as the tempting viand was skillfully withdrawn, followed it and the "retiring maid" down the steps, through the hall, and into the yard.

Four natives of the "Gem of the Sea" were sadly disappointed; they came for an "illegant bit of a scrimmage," and determined to make that cow do what she did not want to do, as well as increase their reward by extraordinary violence; and they would have liked to follow her, and, as they could not make her go in, make her come out against her will, and without the allurement of turnips. Of this satisfaction her incomprehensible behavior had deprived them, and they went away sad and disappointed men. This incident only placed the character of cows on a still more exalted pedestal, and fully justified my confidence.

My friend Weeville had given me specific directions in writing how to feed that cow; exactly how much bran—of which, after some trouble, and a vain attempt to buy a few pounds of it, I had obtained a bag—was to be mixed with a certain proportion of meal; and how often daily this mess, which is probably English for mash, covered with warm water, was to be fed; and about how much hay would fill up the intervals. These instructions were carefully transmitted to the servant who had charge of the dairy, with particular injunctions to carry them out to the letter, and not to deviate from them in the smallest particular.

For several days my new purchase demeaned herself unexceptionably, being quiet and well-behaved; but at the end of about a week she began to bellow, and kept on increasing her complaints daily until they became unendurable. Neighbors put their heads out of windows, evidently meditating dire resolves unless "something were done, and that shortly," whenever I went into the yard to appease her.

What to do was not very clear. When my dog howls I go out and whip him, and he appears to think that is the right thing to do, and stops; but a cow is such a big thing to whip, and she did not seem to be in the least mollified by a few strokes of a stick that I tried. Gratitude for my good opinion should have induced that cow to take a hint from her equine friends and put a "bridle on her tongue," but, instead of doing so, she gave free vent to her feelings, and, in spite of petting or flogging, abusing or praising, made "the air musical." My exalted admiration for her race diminished as sleep fled from my pillow, and murderous thoughts possessed my soul. I seemed to see a dagger "with its handle to my hand," which looked much like a butcher's knife, and there was an estrangement springing up between us that might have terminated fatally had not the Celtic heroine of the turnip adventure reappeared. With the energy peculiar to that sympathetic race, the lady of the kitchen announced, "It was starving, the poor baste was; and if the master would let her feed the crayture all she wanted, there would be no more noise at all, at all." That consent was not long withheld; one more roar removed all scruples of dignity, superior intelligence, and the like, and Biddy fled to the meal-tub. She returned in ten minutes with the biggest tub of mash the cow or myself had ever seen. The former—not Biddy, but the cow—plunged her nose into it nearly to the eyes, and devoured it without once pausing, and then did the like with a replenished dish. My opinion of the intelligence of cows and Biddies was elevated, and I concluded cow-feeding was not my specialty. With those two feeds, or more properly gluts, of mash, comfort returned to my household.

About the time that these events occurred, milkmen had concluded that the lacteal fluid—or what they sold for such—was scarce and valuable, and they raised the price to the rate of twelve cents a quart. Our cow, which had been baptized with the name of Cushy, gave about eleven quarts daily, and as the household only needed six, there was a clear opening for profit to the extent of sixty cents a day. Pure milk is rather a rarity—by which is intimated that it is not universal—in the milkmen's carts in the great city of New York, where that of a watery consistency and cerulean hue is more common than the dull, pale opaque of the real article. In fact, it is said by dairymen that milk just as it comes from the cow is heating—too heating for persons confined to the narrow and unhealthy limits of a city, and should have a little dash of fresh water to take the fire out.

In spite of their convincing arguments, however, an individual was found so little alive to the excellence of the dealer's milky way as to be ready not merely to pay the current price, but to supply his own cans and send for the milk. This opened a magnificent vista; it was the first of the long series of profits that were to flow in one steady stream from the country place or its accompaniments. If one cow yielded a clear daily income of sixty cents, that a hundred or a thousand would yield proportionally more was merely a question in the rule of three.

There was one little matter, however, that somewhat impaired the full measure of this success. The haymakers, or whoever they are that own hay, had raised the price of their goods to keep pace with the price of milk, so that hay was at the moderate rate of two dollars or two dollars and a half a hundred pounds. Moreover, that was an uncommonly intelligent cow, and she used her superior gifts to assure her own comforts, regardless of my feelings or my profits. The hay was stored in a closet under the steps that led down into the yard, and, in spite of every care and contrivance to keep her out, Cushy would open the door, and not only help herself to all she wanted, but throw down armfuls under her feet, and then, like all her dainty race, she would utterly refuse to eat whatever had become dirty. If the door was latched, she pushed the latch up; if bars were placed across, she removed them with her horns; if a rope was used, she broke or stretched it; and if she could not get in otherwise, she would tear the whole away.

After trying many plans, the door was ingeniously hung from the top, so that, as was supposed, it would effectually prevent her unauthorized inroads; but next day it was found at the other end of the yard, having been carried thither on her head. Besides, the amount of hay she ate seemed to have no effect in diminishing the quantity of mash she wanted; rather she appeared to carry into practice the deceptive proposition of the stingy father to his hungry sons—that he who ate the most meat should have the most pie—by demanding more bran the more hay she consumed.

In spite of these drawbacks she was an immense convenience. Her manufactory seemed to work better than more scientific and artificial arrangements, and turned out a more agreeable article than the most skillful chemical milkman. However disgraceful to human nature is the confession, science is no-

A COW. 31

where against a cow. To be sure, she would on wash-days carry a few clothes off the lines, and drag

them around in the most nonchalant and unconcerned way conceivable; would even now and then get her horns mixed up with the lines generally, and pull out half a dozen hooks; but the moment this was done she was entirely satisfied, and would stand perfectly quiet until she was disencumbered. She made more dirt than was altogether sightly, and a man had to be engaged to come daily and remove it.

These various eccentricities added somewhat to her cost, and made it difficult to compute the amount accurately; but, apart from the value of clothes and clothes-lines, her feed cost thirty dollars a month, and the man's attendance six more. So long as she kept on giving twelve quarts a day, there was a clear profit of four cents daily, besides the thorough manuring of the yard, which with farmers is an important point, and would have been more valuable in this instance if it had been possible to grow any thing in it, and had it not been, unfortunately, that, for some unknown reason, not even a spear of grass had ever been willing to exist there.

The quantity of milk, however, soon began to diminish, until, after six weeks, the arrangement with our neighbor had to be discontinued. This reduced the profit, although Cushy still gave more than an abundance for our family, and there would have been a loss had not hay and bran come up to the occasion by coming down in price. The reader, therefore, must call upon the author of "Ten Acres Enough" to determine, by a few algebraical eliminations, whether, if a cow's yield falls off more or less, and her feed diminishes in price considerably, there is a loss or profit, and if so, why so, and how much. For my part, I never could arrive at any satisfactory conclusion except that pure milk and fresh cream were, either combined or separate, very satisfactory.

Cushy had an excellent disposition; she never exhibited but one evil passion, and that was for the meal-tub: she would feed from the hand or a pail, or, in fact, in any way, so long as she was fed enough. Upon this regimen she waxed fat, until it became a serious question whether she would ever again pass out of the doors that it was at first doubtful whether she would enter. Her stomach was of goodly size when she came, and I did not wonder that it occupied so much of her thoughts; but it grew prodigiously, and she had a way of standing still by the hour, with her head under the clothes on the lines, when the sun began to grow hot in the spring, or of lying at full length in their shade, that was evidently conducive to corpulency. When she wanted her meals, which she did not only at frequent intervals, but whenever any one came into the yard, she would go to the kitchen window, and, thrusting forward her head as far as the bars permitted, would "moo" gently to express her wants. If not attended to immediately, she would soon speak louder, and at last would demand food in the most peremptory tone of stentorian bovine lungs. She invariably had her desires gratified, and thus was this interesting evidence of intelligence greatly developed. She had an amusing way of playing with whatever boxes or baskets might be left in the yard, somewhat regardless, to be sure, of their fragile nature; she would carry them on her head round about, and occasionally pin them to the earth with a thrust of her horns; and if she found the stable, which was of wood, close and uncomfortable, she now and then walked out of it through the side, but did these things in so unconscious a way that no one could find fault.

She kept on growing fat and fatter—(to continue her history and somewhat anticipate events)—until summer came, and it was necessary to send her to the country. Then the services of another Irishman, of course, were called into requisition, and he started off from the house with her, early one morning in June, to lead her eight miles to her future home at Flushing. Neither himself nor the cow was heard of again till late that night, when, with startled countenance, he related his adventures to my friend Weeville. He had hardly turned the corner before a butcher rushed out and announced that he wanted to buy that cow. Patrick indignantly refused, true to the aristocratic Irish idea that the employer is always above disposing of any thing; but the butcher was irrepressible, and, pulling out his wallet, offered ninety-five dollars for her; but Pat retorted, "You'll not get the likes of her for ninety-five dollars." This the would-be purchaser mistook for a haggle over price, and demanded how much she would be sold for, when Patrick, breaking away from him with indignation, answered resolutely, "She is not for sale at all, at all, but going to the country for air and grass."

"But it's an awful time I've had with her," he continued, in his narration. "Sure and didn't she lay down with me twelve times, and didn't I think every blessed time that she would niver get up again? Her tongue hung out a yard, in spite of me watering her at every trough along the road. She kept me ever since tin o'clock this very morning, and would stop to rest whenever she felt like it, until I began to think I shouldn't get home till next day."

Thus Cushy exhibited another evidence of her intelligence. As she had heretofore insisted upon being fed whenever she was hungry, she now had, with equal peremptoriness, demanded rest when she was tired. Fat and unaccustomed to travel, she made the Irishman conform to her views of speed, like the superior being she was, knowing well that he was only sent to wait on and accompany her in her journey. She was evidently pleased with the country, being found next morning up to her knees in clover; and, had it not been for the attacks of a gadfly, which she resented furiously, she would have led a perfectly happy life. She certainly was a model animal. My presentiments of success were not mistaken, and I felt almost like claiming, with the modest author of "Ten Acres Enough," that my impressions were never wrong.

PORTRAIT OF A LADY.

CHAPTER II.

A HOUSE, PLANS, AND SPECIFICATIONS.

IF there is any one thing on which I do pride myself more than another, it is my ability to plan and lay out a house. No matter how remarkable the shape of the lot may be, I can always devise an admirable arrangement; and if architecture, not law, had been my fate, the public would have been surprised at my productions. To be sure, chimneys have an inconvenient habit of coming up through windows, and windows of getting in the way of partitions, or locating themselves in odd and unsymmetrical places; sometimes the only passage from the kitchen to the front door, after my plan is completed, will turn out to be through every room on the first floor, and occasionally the stairs will be omitted; but these are matters for the practical builder to correct—the great point is to mark out the general scheme scientifically.

Of course, therefore, the first thing to do toward

building my intended house was to prepare the plans. A large house—a huge pile of wood or brick—is an abomination, and it costs so outrageously (the profit or loss was never out of my mind); but there seems to be a limit in reduction of size that can not be surpassed. I at once proceeded to lay out an admirable plan for a house twenty-four feet square, a neat, nice, cosy, comfortable little cottage; and this is an economical size, because it requires precisely two lengths of board. I arranged for a grand hall through the centre, and a piazza round three sides; there were four rooms on each floor, and it would have been perfection had not the parlor and dining-room proved to be only about seven feet by twelve, which, after some careful measurements, was determined to be rather small.

However, the plan had so many recommendations that I determined to make an effort with it. In my younger days I had passed much time in Connecticut, and had there seen houses of the nicest kind, attractive inside and out, and which were said to cost only a few thousand dollars apiece. A friend of mine, residing on Long Island Sound, had imported one, which came to him cut out, sawed and marked, ready to be put up. So, having determined to try something of the same nature, I inquired the name of the maker, and sent him my plan, requesting an estimate. Instead of returning me an estimate by which I could readily calculate for a little increase of size, the stupid fellow replied that he would come to New York and show me some plans of his own. I wrote a severe letter in answer, saying that I wanted an estimate, not a plan. Since then I have not heard from the gentleman, and believe he is still studying out the beauties of my arrangement, and will, one of these days, come before the world as a great architect on the strength of my abilities.

Not to be put down or deterred, however, I made other plans, some of which had the kitchen outside, some in the basement, and others on the first floor. In one there was a piazza on all sides, in another there was no piazza whatever; some had the servants in the garret, others placed them in the cellar. I was ready to erect an entirely new house, or to convert an old barn that was near the premises into two or three houses. There was nothing that my resources were not equal to, and the drawings would have furnished quite a new stock in trade for a young architect.

My friends gave me their advice. They respectively assured me that I could not live with my kitchen in a wing, and could not exist if it were any where else; that I would be robbed if the servants were in the attic, and robbed and murdered if they were on the ground floor; that no house was worth building unless it were filled in with brick, and that brick filling was a mere waste of money; that it would be hot as an oven if it was not double boarded, or if it was double boarded and not double plastered; that every floor must be deafened, or that the noise overhead would be unendurable, and that deafening would be of no use whatever; that the roof must be of gravel, or it would leak, and if made of gravel it would break the entire building down; that oiling was the true mode of protecting the woodwork, and that nothing whatever but paint would answer; that the natural wood was the most beautiful trimming, and that only stained or painted woodwork was decent; that the proper way was to paper the walls, and that no paper would stick on fresh walls. There was much more equally valuable advice, for which I was exceedingly grateful, and desire again publicly to thank my friends.

While ruminating over these statements and my various different projects, I was struck with the appearance of a neat little house in one of the streets of the village. It was a parallelogram, which is the most practical and economical shape for a house, and had a modest little piazza in front, and a pretty French roof above. The internal arrangement, with such modifications as my superior experience immediately dictated, was absolute perfection. The building was only twenty-four feet by thirty-six, yet there were seven comfortable rooms on the first and second floors, the parlor moderately large, the dining-room long and narrow to suit a dinner-table, and the bed-rooms of admirable proportion. I determined at once, with the heroism of self-control, to abandon my own fancies, and to look and think no farther; but, having completed my modifications, gave them to a draughtsman, to be expressed in builders' signs and particularized with specifications. This event suggested the following beautiful sentiment: It often happens that, while we are roaming over the world to gratify our desires, the precise article for the purpose is at our very doors.

The drawings and specifications were soon made out in gorgeous style; there was a beautiful picture of what the house would look like, with an amount of finish and moulding that did the draughtsman great credit, showing the inside and outside, sections and ground plans, stairs and closets; and the specifications provided how every nail was to be driven, and were completed with a minuteness that would set imposition at defiance. When finished, they were submitted to several builders for estimates.

This happened at a time when, although the inflation of gold had passed its culminating point, labor and materials were at their highest. The builders, smarting under the recollection of unprofitable contracts made on a rising market, were deaf to my eloquent observations on the certainty of a rapid fall in the value of articles at a time when the war was manifestly drawing to a close. They had lost faith not only in the ninety-days' theory of our leading modern statesman, but that the rebellion would die other than a lingering death, and refused obstinately to be convinced. Some of them offered to oversee the work on a commission, by which ingenious arrangement the more they wasted the more they would make. Others charged nearly double what was the fair value, insisting upon allowing for a farther rise in prices. One man was so entirely overcome that, after keeping the plans a month, he returned them secretly, ran away, and was never heard of afterward.

New York being pretty much exhausted by this time, application was made to the carpenters of Flushing. With one exception, they declined the job, as they called it, entirely; but this one put in the lowest estimate that had yet been made, so that the reader will perceive that Flushing contains not merely the finest building-lots and the gentlest cows, but the most intelligent and enterprising carpenters. There was only one difficulty in the way of closing with this proposal, and that was, as he coolly informed me, that he could not finish the house till next winter. Now I wanted a summer residence, not a winter one. The city is a sane man's home in bleak and stormy weather, but in the summer solstice the green fields and fragrant pastures, limpid brooks and shady trees, tempt an equally sane man (meaning myself, of course) into the country. It is true, much time had been wasted over specifications and estimates, especially by the man who ran away, and the spring was pretty well advanced; but that house had to be done by July. So, as it was impossible to accept the services of the intelligent Flushing mechanic, or to make use of the admirably planned Flushing house, it became necessary to cast about for some other means of accomplishing the object.

Over against the eastern end of that barren and crooked point of land known as Cape Cod, which, projecting into the ocean, considers the object of its being accomplished when it protects and shelters the "Hub of the Universe," lie three islands that were, in early days, according to unquestionable tradition, the estate and property of an elderly gentleman who was blessed with three daughters. On his death the ladies are supposed to have divided the property among them. The daughters' names were Anna, Martha, and Naomi, and their names appertain to the islands still. The largest is called Martha's Vineyard, showing that Martha had the good sense to cultivate the luscious fruit, although the strict Puritan customs of those times may have forbidden her enjoying its juice, except, perhaps, in the Puritan way— on the sly. Anna took the next largest island, which from that day has been called Nantookit, or Nantucket, the graceful Anna being vulgarized into the familiar Nan. Naomi's land has since been converted into Nomansland; and well it might, for no man would have been contented with such a portion while brothers carried off the broad acres of the neighboring islands, and few women, except such submissive creatures as Naomis and Cinderellas are popularly supposed to be.

Of this group, Nantucket was once flourishing and populous, with a large tonnage of whalemen, and a goodly population of whaling-men — where money was so plenty and morals so pure that theft was unknown and hackmen charged fair prices. This modern Arcadia, however, was sadly affected by the rapid diminution of whales, was injured by the invention of kerosene, and ruined by the discovery of petroleum, the barbarous names of which had been, until lately, unknown in all that country. Whales tried, for a time, to compete with these innovations, but, finding the effort useless, gave up in disgust, and retired to their northern homes beyond the reach of man. This would have made little difference if ships were used in obtaining petroleum; but, although enthusiasts suppose it comes from the decayed bones of whales that existed when this old world was young, they had been buried "deeper than ever plummet sounded" beneath the accumulations of modern dust; so the whalemen, being useless, were sunk in Charleston Harbor, and the whaling-men sought "green fields and pastures new" in California.

Nan's inheritance went to decay, and her people were our people—that is, they learned to cheat, and the hackmen imitated their fellows. Population diminished, building lots were worthless, and one half the houses were vacant. But the inhabitants were a Scriptural people, and, remembering how the patriarchal tribes, when water and grass became scarce, struck their tents and struck out for better quarters, they pulled down every man his house—and not only that, but every woman her house—and carried them over to the main land. It was at the zenith of this exodus that my troubles culminated, and hearing of a spot where the inhabitants had each a house to sell, and wanting the article myself, without more ado I ordered one to be delivered at Flushing.

It was not necessary to see the new domicile; it was sufficient that it came from Nantucket, the home of purity and truth, and to be put up by a Nantucketan, doubtless a specimen of these qualities. He contracted to pull it down, transport it to Flushing, and erect it on the premises aforesaid, as we lawyers say, by the seventh day of July then next ensuing; and if he failed so to do, then he was to forfeit and pay the sum of ten dollars for each and every day's default and delay over and beyond such day as aforesaid; provided, however, nevertheless, if he finished and completed such house before the first day of July, he was to receive a further sum of ten dollars a day for each day that the same should be so finished and completed before the said last mentioned, to wit, the first day of July then next ensuing. His name was Sille—not silly, as our New York builders would call him if they read those provisions which, I think, do not disgrace my profession, and which of themselves are more than worth, to the reader, the cost of this book.

The contractor soon sent me a rough diagram of the house. It was not exactly according to my views; instead of being an economical parallelogram, it was made up of angles and eccentricities; the architecture was of the conglomerate style, the main building being Doric and the extension Corinthian; the former having a peaked roof so perpendicular that it seemed as if it never would come to a point, and that a fly would have difficulty in maintaining a foothold on it, and the latter being so flat that a ball would hardly roll off the eaves. The whole was ornamented with an unlimited amount of trimming and moulding, and there were windows of all shapes and characters. There was stained glass in the front and rear doors, plain glass in some windows, and parti-colored panes in others; there were windows where no one would expect them, and blanks where one would naturally expect windows. It might have been called a model of surprises. To a person who prided himself on his abilities for laying out a plan economically and advantageously, this was discouraging; but, after all, to a philosophic mind, so long as the necessary accommodation is obtained, the particular plan makes little difference.

Flushing is a small place, and any unusual occurrence throws it into a wild state of excitement.

Some one had been moving a house down its main street in the ordinary manner, with rollers and a windlass, and its slow rate of progression led to much animadversion, and many remarks that in a country village pass for jokes. One by-stander wanted to know whether it had stopped at the corner to take a drink, another desired to inquire whether it was going to the city for a visit, and a third sarcastically pointed out its rate of speed as an example for the railroad company to imitate. The Flushing *Gazette* took the matter up, and had an editorial every week on the progress of the house. So the reader can imagine what was the effect when the Flushingites learned that a stranger was about bringing a house from Nantucket. The *Gazette* entered into the subject with spirited hilarity, hoping that it would move faster than the "pattern house," and wondering whether it would sail down or come by land—suggesting that the other houses, the old settlers, ought to call on the new-comer—and generally made itself quite facetious over the affair.

After signing his agreement, Mr. Sille disappeared, it was supposed, to look up the house, and the foundation was rapidly completed by a resident mason; but neither he nor the house reappeared. Weeks went by; the prophecies of the incredulous were being confirmed; those who had "known better" all along were in high spirits; the evidence was altogether against the success of the new enterprise, and were among the most favorable. It was rumored that contractor, house, and all had gone down in a storm on the Long Island Sound. In the midst of these dreadful rumors, a vessel appeared one morning at the dock near the premises, and landed bricks, beams, and timbers—evidently what had been once a house, and what must be a house again. The whole aspect of affairs changed; hilarity succeeded gloom; doubts disappeared; hopes grew into certainties; and the mason who was building the foundation engaged all the carts, trucks, and wagons in the village to transport what he called "the stuff" to my premises. He drove down in a great state of excitement—only to find the gate to the dock closed and locked.

Here was an unexpected block to the wheels of progress. There was a high, strong gate. On one side, all the vehicles of Flushing; on the other, a mass of timber, joists, boards, and shingles, supposed to represent a house. On careful investigation, it turned out that an Irishman named Barney—whether it was something Barney or Barney something, no one ever knew, as he was invariably called simply

Barney—had hired the dock, and demanded "his damages" before he would allow "the stuff" to leave. Here was a predicament—my house landed, all the transportation of the village ready to remove it, and an obstinate Irishman named Barney barring the way. He was immovable, however, insisting upon "his damages;" so the carts, and wagons, and trucks drove away, and the Irish character came under a lively discussion. The inhabitants of the Emerald Isle are certainly a magnificent race, especially when their biographer does not happen to own a house which has strayed on their land, and does want to run for alderman; and if they did not lie, steal, cheat, rob, murder, get drunk, perjure themselves, quarrel, fight, and insist upon damages unreasonably, they would be almost as good as other nations. Barney was evidently a superior Irishman, and, as no one had ever landed a load of house at his dock before, and probably never would again, he felt that the dignity of tenants was at stake, and must be sustained.

When these facts were reported to me I took down my law-books, and prepared a rod for Mr. Barney. There was the clear right to land at a public dock; there was the clear wrong of detaining property belonging to another. Damages began to loom up before my eyes, and a very pretty case as introduction to a lucrative legal practice in the place of my newly-intended residence. Vistas of writs, and suits, and appeals, and new trials, rose in my mind in graceful array, and I thanked Barney, who was reported to be not only "ugly," but responsible, with all my heart. There were two difficulties in the way of legal action—first, that until the suit was terminated the residence could not be built; secondly, that Sille, who would have to be plaintiff, had disappeared from the sight of man. Now the house might be delayed, as the damages would thus be increased; but a suit without a plaintiff was beyond ordinary legal remedies, and was not provided for even by the new Code of Procedure. So Barney, Irishman-like, in spite of law, justice, sense, or hospitality, kept my house, or rather intended house, by "force and arms," and the cellar and foundation were completed alone.

A cellar is a delightful part of a house, it is so cool in summer and warm in winter; it is such a nice place to store "things," as the housewives call them; but to have all cellar and no house is carrying the point too far. It is a pleasant place when surmounted by the proper amount of beams and mortar, but alone is like an alligator's countenance, altogether too open. I am not particular, and could have made out during the summer months, probably, if the cellar had only been upside down.

The foundation was built, the mason was out of work, and myself out of humor, when we were both again raised to the pinnacle of happiness by the arrival of another vessel, which fortunately selected another dock, and landed another house. On inquiry, it appeared that this was my house. Lest the reader may suppose that Nantucket was so overflowing with houses that they floated down the Sound and drifted ashore any where, it must be explained that the first house was merely the workshop. So the carts and trucks reappeared, and this time carried away the *débris* of what was once the house of some bluff seafaring man—timbers that were shivered, as he had no doubt often requested they should be, doors, windows, shingles, pieces of roof, floor-boards, posts, moulding, and a thousand other odds, ends, bits, and pieces, in the most admired confusion—and deposited them upon my entire five acres, scattered hither and thither, as though they were component parts of five houses instead of one.

As Mr. Sille had not come with the house, but was to arrive the next day—for it appeared he had been storm-bound in some of the numerous "bights," as the Yankees call them, of Nantucket or Martha's

Vineyard—he sent a watchman who was to sleep among the "stuff," and prevent Mr. Barney's compatriots from converting it into firewood.

Mr. Sille was to arrive the next day. Week after week went by, but he did not appear. The house lay on the ground as though a hundred-pound rebel shell had dropped into the cellar and scattered it to the four winds of heaven; the watchman waited, watched, and prayed, doubtless, for relief, till his money was spent, and his shoes worn out, and his coat threadbare; I alternated between imbecility and fury; Barney even was overcome, and sent word begging to have the workshop, which had been placed on top of a pile of his hay, removed; and Flushing made it the regular fashionable evening drive to visit my five acres to see how the house was—not getting on.

In about a month, when the mason had almost become crazy, myself frantic, and Barney idiotic, Sille reappeared from Nantucket or some other remote spot, looking like the ghost of his former self, and announced that he had been at the point of death. Not taking into consideration for a moment my losses and sufferings, he absolutely wanted sympathy; in the first place, he must nearly drown himself, and now he must catch the erysipelas, and expect me to feel for any one but myself. I asked him sternly

whether this was his habit with every house that he moved, and explained that it must not happen again; that I had been sick too—very sick of the whole affair; that the watchman had become demoralized and run away; that it was nearly midsummer, and that all Flushing was laughing at us.

The watchman lived in a little place not larger than a good-sized dog-kennel that he constructed from pieces of roof, and the boys of the neighborhood considered it fine sport to pay him a visit of a dark night, and signalize their presence by a shower of stones. His food was never luxurious, being cooked by himself under many disadvantages and with few utensils; and when his money became scant, it was supplied mainly through the charity of the neighbors. He had no bedding and no change of clothes; and when a murder was committed near by, and the murderer was hunted through the place by constables, officers, and half the people as *posse comitatus*, accompanied by all the dogs in the village; and the crowd, yelling, screaming, and fighting, rushed over the watchman's kennel at midnight, waking him out of sleep, he could stand it no longer, but incontinently fled to parts unknown; so that Sille had not arrived too soon, and found every thing needing care and attention. He went to work at once, and, bringing order out of chaos, began rapidly to construct the confused mass of material into the form and stature of a dwelling.

Murders are abhorrent things to me; either from some natural idiosyncracy, or from the training of my profession, which teaches obedience to the powers that be, and prefers technicalities to violence, I have a positive objection to murdering any one or being murdered myself—especially the latter. It is so dirty and bloody, the body is so dreadful to look at and so hard to dispose of, and the whole affair so sudden and altogether unpleasant. I was anxious to know, before settling in Flushing, whether murder was one of the institutions, and was to be guarded against like chills and fever, musquitoes, and other similar visitations

A day or two after the occurrence, I applied to my invaluable friend Weeville for information, and inquired whether murders were a common event in that neighborhood. His manner in reply was very encouraging. He had lived in Flushing nine years, and this was the first case of the kind. It was the most peaceable place he knew; in fact, he had hardly ever heard a loud word spoken. He pictured it as the abiding-place of angels or Quakers, and put my scruples entirely at rest. Violence, or disputes even, among the Flushingites were not heard of, and murders were far rarer than deaths by lightning.

The day after this conversation there was a little friendly contest among various fire-companies at the peaceable village to determine which engine could throw the highest stream of water; and what was my amazement, on reading the accounts in the daily papers, to learn that the contest wound up in a free fight; that knives, pistols, and clubs were freely used, and that four persons were killed and forty wounded. For a family of semi-angels this was doing well. The philosophy of averages furnished one consolation, however—Flushing had evidently concentrated into one day its allowance of murders for the next five years.

None of Sille's men were in the fight, although at first I anticipated finding my cellar a hospital, and expected a renewed experience in the matter of lint and bandages, such as occupied so much of our time during the war. He kept on steadily adding boards, and windows, and siding, and beams together, till they took on the semblance of a house. To be sure, it was rickety and open as yet: one man fell between the timbers, another out of a window, and a third from the roof—but that did not hurt the house.

Two Irishmen were one day at work digging a well, and I commenced moralizing at their fate—doomed to a lower existence than hewers of wood and drawers of water, not sufficiently intelligent, even, to cut sticks, and condemned to carry wood and dig for water; their life one of weary, heart-rending, back-breaking toil; no time for pleasure, no chance to cultivate the intellect and develop the mind—a miserable life, little better than death itself.

Musing on their hard lot, I peered down into the

deep hole they were making in the ground during the intense heats of summer, wondering how soon science would raise the lowest of men above the condition of beasts of burden, when one of them, glancing up, perceived me, and inquired, "Was I the boss?" I answered in the affirmative, and he informed me that it was customary for the boss to "stand something" when he first came on the ground. Moved by my sympathies, I stood a dollar apiece, explaining that it must not be wasted in liquor, to which they assented with great hilarity. Alas for sympathy, and charity, and the milk of human kindness! those wretched men immediately clubbed their two dollars together, and, converting them into gin, knocked off work and proceeded to get drunk. They remained incoherent, as the term goes that is applied to their betters, all the next day. As it was essential that the well should be finished as rapidly as possible, my feelings changed, my sympathy died a premature death, and I never stood any thing of the kind again.

What with drunken Irishmen and injured workmen, murdered villagers and fighting firemen, the country house progressed slowly toward completion. The walls, it is true, arose like mushrooms—those delicious vegetables, which I must pause to compliment —in a night; the roof climbed into place, partitions grew and floors were laid, windows crept into their sash-cases, and doors and blinds were hung, but "the end was not yet." The seventh day of July had come and gone, and the country house bid fair to be finished about Christmas time.

Of the cost of the progressing dwelling it is not pleasant to speak; but as this veritable history depends greatly, for its value to future generations, upon its accuracy and minuteness, I will admit the expense was not despicable. Labor was high, as the Nantucket builder explained, and timber was high, and bricks were high, and Irishmen occasionally got high, and altogether he was compelled—much against his wishes—to charge a high price. As the building progressed, or rather failed to progress, it was suggested that he may have charged enough to leave a surplus to cover a few days' delay at ten dollars a day; but that would hardly have accorded with the proverbial honesty of Nan's dower island.

I concluded to hire a house near by, which, although not the one I expected to occupy, was doubtless as good, and had the advantage of a tight roof and solid walls. Here I could conveniently watch the progress of the undertaking without being so deeply interested as if my lodging depended on it. As distance is supposed to lend enchantment to the view, the distant prospect of the completion of my house should have been enchanting; and as summers invariably return every year, it would be only a question of a few months, and my summer house would be merely a next summer house.

CHAPTER III.

MORE LIVE-STOCK—A HORSE AND A PIG. WHICH IS THE NOBLER ANIMAL?

IN order to live in the country, one must own a horse; in order to keep house in the country, one must own a pig. In popular estimation, the animal creation stand in relation to man in the following order—cows, horses, pigs, dogs. For the existence of a large portion of the race of infants in these modern days of tight lacing and slender limbs, a cow is a prime necessity; for utility in transferring one's self from place to place between which there is no railroad, or if there is, and the person's life is precious in his own eyes, a horse is extremely useful; for association in contemplative moments and suggestiveness of comfortable ideas, a pig is very pleasant; for the higher enjoyments of life, for the sports of the field and wood, the dog takes first rank.

I have already described the cow. My dog, like those of all my friends, is the best in the world, and

I bought the "love of a pig." Pigs are a highly intellectual race; they not only know on which side their bread is buttered, but in which part of the trough to find the best-buttered pieces. Reader, didst thou ever study the language of a pig—the beautiful intonations of its various expressions; the grunt of welcome at its master's approach; the sharp warning to desist if punishment is threatened; the squeal demanding more food, broken often into the most piteous accents of entreaty; the cry of pain, or scream of rage? Pig-language is a copious one, although the power to understand it is given to but few of the human race. The expressions of a pig's face are most impressive; the eye speaks the enjoyment of a joke—twinkles with fun, as we say; conveys an intimation of anger, or expresses scorn of an underhand action or watchfulness against it. Who ever got the better of a pig by fair means? Chase him, and see him provokingly keep half a dozen feet ahead of you; try to drive him, and measure his obstinacy even by that of your wife; endeavor to lead him, and make up your mind to have a "good time."

Our pig united many pleasant qualities and points of sagacity to a gentleness and suavity rare in the race; he had an appetite that was a joy to behold, and was as effective an appetizer as a gin-cocktail.

MORE LIVE-STOCK. 63

The household was large, and swill consequently abundant, but piggy never shrank from his duty; he seemed to feel that the reputation of all pigdom rested on him, and, no matter how often the trough was replenished, he was ever ready to renew his attacks. His sides were puffed out and rounded like a ball, but he would stand with one foot in the trough, and never desist till the last morsel was consumed. He was as clean and white as a baby in a morning-gown, and would allow his flanks to be scratched in the most gracious way, grunting gently the while, and occasionally turning over on his side. He was altogether a rarely sociable companion: so much for our pig.

In selecting a horse, there was one point I had made up my mind upon—he must be gentle; he might be fast or slow, stylish or commonplace, but kind in single or double harness, as the professionals term it, he should be. My experience of horse-flesh has been varied and instructive: I have been thrown over their heads and slid over their tails; have been dragged by saddle-stirrups and tossed out of wagons; I have had them to balk and to kick, to run and to bolt, to stand on their hind feet and kick with their front, and then reciprocate by standing on their front and kicking with their hind feet. I have seen more of a horse's heels, have known more of the intricacies and possibilities of a "smash-up," have had more bits of pole and whiffle-trees sent flying over my head than falls to the lot of most men; I have been thrown much with horses, and more by them; I have had them do nearly every thing they should not have done, and leave undone all that they should have done. So gentleness was the one prerequisite to a purchase, and many were the animals I examined to secure this qualification, many the faults I discovered; but I finally obtained the precise creature I wanted. He was graceful, free, fast, stylish, and, above all, perfectly gentle—a very family horse.

On the confines of Flushing stands a house about two hundred feet from the road, and surrounded on three sides by a high hedge of *arbor-vitæ*. At the front is a court-yard, and what was once a stately entrance, with a carriage-drive round a circle, and a number of noble forest-trees; but the grass has covered the carriage-road, weeds have choked the lawn, and the trees spread their scraggy branches untrimmed and uncared for. The dwelling is large, and has a deep piazza along the entire front; it gives every outward appearance of comfort, but no family has occupied it more than two consecutive months for many years. The house is haunted.

Many years ago an old French lady owned the place, and she had one daughter—a beauty, of course —given to falling in love, equally of course, or she would not have been French—and somewhat undutiful, as the sequel will show. The mother, according to the ordinary Parisian habit, wished to make a good match for her daughter; the latter, according to the universal female habit, wished to select a handsome husband for herself; the mother offered a wealthy and highly respectable "mentor, guide, and friend" of sixty; the young lady chose a dashing, devil-may-care lover of twenty-five. The parent dismissed the latter, the daughter dismissed the former; the mother threatened to anathematize if she was not obeyed, and, being disobeyed, did something of the kind—what, among gentlemen, would be called "tall swearing." The daughter, who had learned the habits of American children, consented to an elopement with her lover; the time was set, the hour arrived.

It was a bright moonlight night, the seventh of October, in the year eighteen hundred and no matter what; a high wind was blowing, and scattered clouds were driving rapidly across the sky; the young gentleman at the appointed hour stood at the gate with a pair of fast trotters and one of the lightest turn-outs of Brewster & Co., of Bond Street, having engaged a clergyman in the city of New York. Time flew by, but he waited in vain. His lady-love had not failed of her promises, however, but, after her mother had retired, and by her loud snoring attested the profundity of her repose, she quietly descended the stairs, opened the front door silently as the expertest of thieves, and stepped upon the piazza. At that moment a heavy cloud passed across the moon, and a fierce gust slammed to the door; fearing that her mother might have been aroused, she groped her way hastily across the piazza, caught the balustrade of the steps, and—walked off on the wrong side. It was a fall of ten feet; with a wild shriek she pitched head foremost on the bricks of the area.

The lover waited and waited, fearing let suspicions might have been aroused, or resolution have failed; amid the noise of blustering winds and falling leaves he thought he heard a cry of distress, and, at last becoming uneasy, determined to visit his dulcinea's window, and ask her how she did. Tying his horses, he crept quietly along the shady side of the hedge, which was that on the opposite side to her room, as he did not wish to be seen. As soon as he reached the piazza, he followed along under the edge of it till he came to the steps, where he waited for a friendly cloud to conceal his movements, when he was compelled to pass outside of them.

The opportunity soon offered, he slipped by, and the cloud cleared away just after he had stumbled on a bundle of clothes, as he supposed, beyond the steps; he turned to look; and there, lying upon her back, staring up to heaven with lack-lustre, wide-open eyes, the crimson stains upon her white forehead telling her fate, stiff, and stark, and cold, lay all that he held dearest in this world. Her lips would never again whisper words of love; her heart had ceased to feel that passion which had proved her destruction. The lover's cries aroused the house, and brought out the trembling mother to behold her daughter still undisturbed, with the horror of sudden and cruel death upon her unmitigated. And amid the shrieks of the parent and the lamentations of the servants, the maddened lover, who had been attacked with a frenzy that never left him, heaped reproaches, and retaliated with curses on her whose curses seemed in his insanity to have caused this terrible calamity.

Of the parties to this tragedy there were none living in three months; they were buried in adjoining graves, at the request of the mother, who had it done apparently as an atonement. This palliation did not seem to answer, however, for on the seventh of every month, at the hour of eleven, a ghostly figure slips out of the front door, whether it is locked or not, and with a scream falls from the piazza; a male figure suddenly appears rent with agony at its side, and then another female wringing her hands in despair, while the male gesticulates fiercely at her. Such is this veritable history as I have it from the oldest inhabitant, and it is no wonder that people do not like living in a house with such associates.

I do not often use our horse; I am not fond of driving, and have a vivid recollection of the early accidents with horse-flesh heretofore mentioned; but when it became necessary to buy a pig, my judgment was indispensable, and I was compelled to drive to the place of his residence—which was the haunted house. I did not know that it was haunted, and, being well aware of the decorum that requires the master of the establishment to "tool" his coachman, no matter how much more competent the latter may be, I took the reins, and dashed in grand style along the entrance to the door. Leaving the coachman at the animal's head, I walked to the pig-pen, which was in the rear of the house, and there was soon engrossed in admiring the beautiful little creature that I have already described. Many minutes were devoted to the contemplation of his innumerable fine points, and I was only aroused by the noise of a struggle, shouts for help, and a clatter of hoofs. Instantly running toward the front, I arrived just in time to see the heels of Dandy Jim—for such was the animal's name—disappearing round the corner, and to help my groom, who was lying on his back in the road, upon his feet.

It seemed that the horse had stood perfectly quiet for several minutes, then became uneasy, began to tremble, and turn his head with a wild look over his shoulder. In spite of the efforts of the coachman, who was a powerful fellow, and had been severely bruised in the struggle, he reared and plunged violently, and finally, breaking away, dashed round the circle, out at the entrance, and away up the road. The man firmly believed that Dandy had seen the ghost, which was now mentioned for the first time, although my views inclined to accept the occurrence as an outcropping of the original sin of the horse family.

The pursuit of a runaway horse is a melancholy operation—his speed is so much greater than his pursuer's; his means of flight so much better than the latter's opportunities for stopping him; he has four feet to set against two, and knows so well how to use them; he has such unpleasant soundness of wind and limb, and such a raging devil inside of him, while the satisfaction of recovering ruined *débris* is so slight, and the mode of punishment so vague. I followed along as best I might, picking up a cushion here, a blanket there, the whip in one place, and the seat in another, inquiring of every one that I met whether they had seen a horse, and being invariably answered "that they guessed they had." It is enough to say that, after smashing every thing to pieces, tearing the body of the wagon from the wheels, tossing out what was movable, and ruining his harness,

Dandy Jim became satisfied, and allowed a rustic to catch him.

Here was a pretty family horse—afraid of a ghost when all respectable families teach their children that there are no such things as ghosts; running away under supernatural, and without even the excuse of mortal, terror. I felt like shooting or selling —probably the latter, on economical principles— Dandy Jim, but eventually concluded to repair, or, more properly, remake the wagon. I could only have sold out at a great loss—and I so rarely rode behind him.

Dandy had several peculiarities of temper besides his fear of ghosts. He did not like steam-engines— if he had known how many people they kill, he would have been entirely justifiable; so one day, when I was crossing the track after having been to make a visit to a friend—for no one visits on foot in the country —Dandy Jim saw the engine approaching. That was sufficient; he immediately rose on his hind legs and pawed the air. This might possibly have contented him, but the leather straps, which were not intended to stand such a strain, gave way, and the wagon came upon his heels. What then happened I do not precisely know; he seemed to fly; occasionally he would appear to rise above the trees, and then to descend into the bowels of the earth; he leaped from side to side of the road with an ease and rapidity that would have shamed a well-practiced kangaroo; the wagon bounded after him like the tail to a boy's kite when the latter gets pitching about with the violence of the wind, while his heels played like flashes of lightning far over my head. Fortunately, a countryman ran to my assistance and held back the wagon, while another caught the horse by the head. I rewarded those men liberally. Now a family horse should not kick, nor plunge, nor rear.

Another of his peculiarities was a dislike to standing. He did not mind standing in the stable in the least, but when he was harnessed he expected to keep moving. I hardly drove him sufficiently to learn his eccentricities of temper, and on one occasion laid down the reins for a moment. He immediately started, and the reins slipped over the dash-board out of reach. Reader, have you ever experienced the feeling of being run away with—I mean, female reader—by a horse? If not, do not aspire to it. It is not pleasant. The motion is rapid, and perhaps exhilarating, but it is not smooth, and the mode of stopping is uncertain. There is little to do, and probably much to suffer, with a possibility of ceasing to be. Dandy, instead of being a family horse, ought to have been a race-horse; his speed was wonderful, though I forgot to time it. I held by the dash-board, and shouted "ho!" at the top of my voice. Evidently his knowledge of English was imperfect; he mistook "ho" for "go," and the more I shouted the faster he went.

Where we went, or how we went, I never knew. When I came to my ordinary senses, and escaped from what seemed to me like a blazing comet on a "bust," I found myself on the top of a pile of soft dirt—that species of filth that the farmers obtain in

the city, and put on their lands to make vegetables grow. Although it smelled strong, and my clothes were seriously damaged, my body proved, on careful examination, to be unhurt, and my mental nature only badly scared. I concluded to sell that family horse. My prejudices and impressions were in this instance, as in all others, borne out by the result. I determined to wait, before I drove again, till I could drive my own private steam-engine, for, with good management, I believe steam-engines run smoother than horses.

It is hardly necessary to mention other peculiarities, such as an insane desire to eat me up whenever I passed near his head, in entire disregard of the fact that Nature had not made him carnivorous, and an equally intense wish to kick me with his heels whenever I passed by his flanks. These idiosyncracies prevented my visiting the stable frequently, while our out-door acquaintance he had made short, and not sweet. Fortunately, he was lame most of the time, and when he was not lame he wanted shoeing, so that the family were not able to risk their lives unreasonably often.

All this while the pig had been quietly feeding and growing; in fact, a pig is a very different sort of animal. A pig never runs away and smashes wag-

ons; a pig never kicks people, nor dashes out their brains, nor drags them by stirrups, nor does other such disagreeable things, but is gentle and sweet tempered; he is all good. A boar's head was the famous dish of antiquity; his hams, and shoulders, and sides enable nations to carry on war, ships to go to sea, and commerce to exist; his bristles help us to keep our heads and clothes clean; his skin bestrides his competitor—and then, upon the classic rule of a part standing for the whole, he is in his right place;

his petitoes are the delight of connoisseurs; his entrails are converted into delicious sausages; and who has not read the apotheosis of roast pig? Of a horse, the hide and bones perhaps are useful, but the worthless carcass is only fit for carrion; dangerous in life, while in death his boiling bones breed a pestilence.

Which, then, is the nobler animal?

NOTE.—My horse has just run away again, and I must go and collect the wagon.

CHAPTER IV.

THE COUNTRY, AND HOW TO GET THERE.

A VERY large portion of every man's life is expended in transporting himself from one place to another, and there are several modes of doing it. The most disagreeable and disgusting is to crowd into a city railroad car, and the next is to ride in an omnibus; the dyspeptic rich use carriages, the healthy poor do not; you can go on horseback if you know how to stay there and your horse is agreeable; in cold weather skating is rapid, in warm weather steam-boats carry you luxuriantly; and, if time is an object, and life is none, you trust yourself to the locomotive. To reach Flushing, you must use both steam-boat and railroad.

"There is one thing," said Weeville, in the commencement of our enterprise, with his usual enthusiastic manner, "that you will appreciate—the access to Flushing is most convenient; there are twelve trains each way daily, and they run with perfect regularity. No railroad in the country is so well managed as ours, and no trip could be pleasanter. You have a half hour on the ferry-boat, and almost twenty minutes in the cars, just a delightful variety and absolute safety. Why, they have never killed a passenger since the track was laid."

This was certainly satisfactory information, and I had to regret that the necessity of repairing this admirable road compelled its intelligent and exemplary managers to reduce the number of trains considerably the very day I commenced building. But it was certainly time the repairs were made, as a train had just broken through a bridge, and commenced the customary business of killing passengers; and the entire pile-work, which constitutes one half the track, was discovered to be utterly rotted out. I was not sorry the repairs were commenced, although I was sadly inconvenienced, as the speed and regularity had apparently both decayed with the wood-work.

Compared with other places, the superior accessibility of Flushing was apparent. The delay would be temporary, and for good purpose; whereas, if you wish to live on the North River, it is an even chance that you are dumped into the water every day or two; if you travel by the Long Island road, you must carry a month's provision, and carefully avoid standing on the platforms or sitting in the front car—collisions, at the moderate speed of this road, rarely affect the rear cars; if you are on the line of the Erie, or Morris and Essex, you will have to clamber over Bergen Hill, and take the train after it comes out of the tunnel, provided you desire an approach to safety; and the weight and inconvenience of a life-preserver on a hot summer day—even one of the patent portable blow-up-able vests of modern invention—render steam-boat travel unendurable. In going to Flushing you have a double cause for rejoicing—you are first thankful when you are safe off the steam-boat and on board the cars, and, in returning, doubly thankful when you are safe out of the cars and back again on the steam-boat.

There is an unreasonable prejudice in the public mind against being killed on a railroad. There are many worse deaths: there is hanging, for instance, but that, alas! is rare, or we should have fewer aldermen; there is being broken on the wheel on the French antique model, or sawed asunder after the Chinese fashion; lockjaw is unpleasant, apoplexy uncomfortable, and epilepsy repulsive. In fact, death is so disagreeable, and comes in so many ways, that a man hardly knows how to make a judicious choice.

Therefore I always sit on the end seat, provided the ladies, as is their artless habit, bless their souls! have each occupied a bench to herself, and have thus taken up all the room, for I would as lief any time face death as a strange woman with a hoop-skirt. Besides, by so doing I have a monopoly of this bench myself, and, if I am to be killed, have it done out of hand and without prolonged inconvenience.

The Flushing cars were crowded, which proves what a thriving place it was, for the gentlemanly directors would certainly never willingly inconvenience or unnecessarily crowd their passengers; and the dépôt is not skillfully constructed. Alongside the platform was the track of the Long Island road, beyond it a narrow strip of two or three boards, and then the Flushing track. As the Long Island train was always in, or coming in, or going out when the Flushing train was about to start, much practice, nerve, and courage were required to reach it safely. The other train had either to be stormed or avoided; passengers had to dribble in a long line between the tracks, or climb over the platform of the Long Island cars; and, since no one insulted them by gratuitous advice, they not unfrequently took the wrong train.

As nerve, courage, and presence of mind are valuable qualities, and rarely cultivated among ladies,

Hunter's Point dépôt was equal to a public school, and deserved the commendation of the public. No man or woman who has safely traveled by this road for a year need dread "the battle or the breeze." Any one who can stand on a platform not more than two feet wide, and, unmoved, let one train whiz past in one direction and another whiz past in the contrary, without allowing dress or person to be caught or struck, deserves a diploma for self-command. Of course, a few "go under" in learning how, but the mass of the traveling public is vastly improved by the experience.

The completion of the repairs of the road was not followed by an immediate return to traditional punctuality. I remember reaching Hunter's Point one evening by the Twenty-third Street ferry "just in time to be too late;" the train did not wait for the boat, which was delayed because the pilot had a curious incapacity for steering into the dock, and usually ran against all the pile-work of the neighborhood. The train went out of the dépôt as I came into it. There was only an hour to wait, however, and a person should never be without that amount of patience; so I sat down on the platform, dangling my feet over the edge, as was the universal custom, and commenced to endure an hour's unnecessary existence. It is queer how we hate life when it is forced upon us, and how we love it when there is danger of its being taken away from us. There sat half a dozen men who would have given from five to fifty dollars each to have had sixty minutes less of life, whereas the wretch on the scaffold would give five thousand for sixty minutes more.

The hour went by, then another, and another, each bringing accessions to the crowd of anxious, hungry, unhappy waiting men and women that clung round the dépôt like drones round a hive, and giving me plenty of time to work out the foregoing speculations. Night came upon us. The only official—the ticket-man—shut up his office and went home, probably to a loving wife and family; the brakeman put out all but one light; five o'clock had resolved itself into ten. Conveyances of all kinds, from a carriage down to a swill-cart, were in demand to carry passengers to Flushing; fares by these novel and somewhat dilatory vehicles ranged from one dollar to five. Men became disgusted, women exhausted, and children irrepressible; but still no train. When I left in despair, at about midnight, the men had fallen asleep on the benches, while women were frantically demanding where there was a respectable hotel.

Next day it appeared that the train had run off

the track. On this road the engine had, in those early days of its unperfected existence, the habit of running with one end foremost while going, and with the other end foremost when returning; so that, as it unfortunately is not provided with a cow-catcher at both extremities, it occasionally met with difficulties. On this particular occasion, during the return trip, a stupid ox had planted himself in the way, entirely forgetting that the cow-catcher was not there for him, and absolutely succeeded in discommoding and annoying at least five hundred people, besides killing himself—a piece of stupidity on his part only worthy of an ox.

The trains had become very variable; during the first week of my residence in Flushing, out of the six trips four were failures, and in the first month I had completed the round of experiences. The boat had missed the train, and the train had missed the boat; the boat had blown or burnt up—I never knew which —and the train had gone off the track. Several men who were not experienced in dodging had been killed; fuel had given out, and water dried up; engines had grown wheezy, and bridges become rickety; the pilot had run down the dock entirely, and the engine reduced its speed to six miles an hour. Once the train started before the time, but the outsiders became so enraged that no train ever afterward started on time; in fact, every conceivable mode of evading punctuality had been tested, but I was happy, at the conclusion, to be able to repeat the immortal words, "I still live."

Philosophy is a great resource under such circumstances, and, after all, there is often as much gained as lost by a want of punctuality. Many a comfortable nap and undisturbed perusal of the daily papers—two pleasures for which the ordinary day rarely furnishes opportunities—have I had by the aid of the Flushing Railroad. Some persons grumbled, and abused the officials, and uttered bad language, but it did no good. The employés soon became used to the disappointment, why should not the passengers? On one occasion, when the locomotive had been wheezing along at a snail's pace, stopping frequently to rest and take breath, I became alarmed, and asked a brakeman what was the matter with the engine. This was temerity on my part, for railroad men do not approve of familiarity from passengers, and I dreaded the result as he gazed calmly at me; but suddenly a smile broke over his countenance, and he answered laconically, "Played out."

The conductor was another sort of man; when an unhappy passenger, who had not borne his trials well, and during the summer had uttered numerous complaints, was finding fault toward the close of the season with some omission or commission, the conductor, whose patience had been entirely exhausted, turned upon him with,

"You have been casting slurs on our railroad all summer; now what do you know about it?"

"Why, I have been spending the season at Flushing, and have been traveling on it."

"Then let me tell you, it is as well managed as other railroads, and if you don't like it you need not ride on it. I don't want any passengers who are not satisfied."

This was putting things on their true basis; some silly people think it a swindle when certain times are advertised but not kept, when boats are taken off without notice, connections are not made, and the time of passengers is wasted; but they seem to forget that they need not go by rail. If they do not wish to ride, they can always walk; the choice is open to them, and Flushing is only six miles off.

NOTE.—Since the foregoing was written all this has been changed. The railroad has been put in charge of a newspaper editor. It now has the finest cars, the best conductors, and makes the most regular time of any road in the United States. My lots are not all sold yet.

CHAPTER V.

A WELL.

"If 'twere well done when 'twere done, 'twere well 'twere done quickly."

SOME of the incidents connected with digging our well have already been referred to, but good water is so necessary to a country place that the mode of obtaining it deserves a separate chapter. Well-digging is a profession, and the most cultivated master of the art to be found in the neighborhood had been engaged, immediately after the foundation of the house was commenced, to dig the well. It was strange, however, how many people at about the same time had determined to do the same thing; it seemed as though the entire village had been seized with a mania for sinking wells. He was exceedingly busy, and was compelled, much against his wishes, to demand an exorbitant price for his services. He regretted it deeply, but he would have to ask four dollars and a half a foot. As the ordinary price was about a dollar, it was certainly honest of him to explain beforehand the necessities of his situation;

A WELL.

and although it was inconvenient that the villagers should have been stricken with this fancy at so inopportune a moment, it was certainly fortunate that the man was so honest. He was employed at once, and strongly impressed with the necessity of the utmost haste.

It is probable that his other engagements engrossed much of his time. The well did not progress rapidly; but, as it soon appeared that the house would not be completed for occupation before the ensuing summer, the immediate necessity for drinking-water was done away with. There is a wonderful romance about the "old oaken bucket." Many a time in youthful days have I plunged my nose into its liquid contents, and choked myself, and poured the water down my shirt-front, in frantic endeavors to drink from its thick rim; often have I lowered the empty vessel far into the bowels of the earth, and jumped it up and down at the risk of dashing it to pieces against the stone sides, in order to fill it, and then puffed over the heavy pull of bringing it, laden with the cooling crystal, to the surface. With due reverence have I studied the many poetical things which have been said in its honor; but the days of oaken buckets are numbered; they have been succeeded by force-pumps, and chain-pumps, and iron pumps, that save the muscles, but offend the sensibilities.

Were it not that I was subject to the dominion of several Irish maidens, denominated servants, I should certainly have sacrificed utility to beauty; but, under the force of a ukase from them, I was compelled to buy a pump. Of the various patterns of these, a pretty iron one had taken my fancy, and no sooner was the well completed than it was purchased. Unfortunately, the entire village of Flushing was then putting in pumps, and there was no possibility of having it set up for two entire weeks. We had just occupied the house opposite, which had no well, and we depended for water upon our own.

Reader, have you ever hauled up water from a well in a pail? If you have not, you should learn to do it; it requires skill and courage. You must balance yourself carefully on a few loose planks, and, peering down giddily into the dark hole that yawns beneath, you must lower the pail with a long rope for what seems an endless distance, and when it reaches the bottom, will have to jerk it about vigorously, as it obstinately refuses for a long time to fill; and then you must draw up carefully the heavy weight that threatens to pull you in, instead of your pulling it out; and manage not to let it touch the sides, as that will spill the contents. All the while the slipping of board, or earth, or foot will necessitate the calling together of a coroner's jury.

It is a pity that there is no way of falling down a well comfortably. If you go down head foremost, your feet stick out above the water, it is true, but you do not breathe through that portion of the body; if you strike feet foremost, the climb back is such a long and uncertain journey; and if you go down doubled up, you are apt to find trouble in straightening out. Every time a maid went to the well I speculated as to which of these modes she would follow, and feared that the case of the broken pitcher would be illustrated.

This state of things lasted some time, as the pump-maker found his Flushing customers more exacting than even he expected; or possibly his workmen had gone on more sprees than he allowed for. Three weeks had gone by, and we were still drawing water; and, what is more, the water which we did with such infinite pains draw up was far from good. We had been warned that for some time after its completion the well would be dirty; that before it was finished one or more Irishmen would have to work waist deep in the water, which would not recover from their presence for a long while; but, instead of improving, it became worse and worse. At first it tasted badly, but it soon smelt unendurably. There was a great deal of house-cleaning and washing to do, but the women finally rebelled, and flatly refused to use the odoriferous stuff any longer, even for such base purposes, and it had been from the first utterly undrinkable.

Weeville had always boasted of the purity of the water-bed that underlay this entire tract of land, and in his comparisons had placed it a long way ahead of the Croton. Of course he was called in. "It was useless to tell him any thing against the water; he was not going to believe any visionary stories originated by Irish servant-girls—he must taste it." This he did not do, however; the smell was enough.

"Pheugh!" he burst forth as it approached his nose. "I will tell you what is the matter—the well has never been cleaned out; that infernal well-digger has taken advantage of you, and left the pieces of dirt and rubbish that fall in—old bits of dinner, fragments of meat and cheese, perhaps—and which must always be removed, or they will decay, and spoil the water for a long time."

I immediately went after the well-digger in an intense state of wrath, and rated him soundly for his conduct; but he not only swore by all that was truthful that he had cleaned out the well, but called up the man that did it. A severe cross-examination having convinced me that they both told the truth, I returned home wondering how long it would take to learn to like stinking, as the Mississippians have learned to like dirty, water. I have always had a weakness for water. Whisky is the natural American drink; lager bier is admirably suited to the Teutonic mistinesss of intellect; the frothy Champagne is adapted to the volatile Frenchman, and the thick ale to the muddled Englishman. Brandy is suitable for men, if we are to believe high authority. Gin, in the shape of schnapps, was the daily potation of our respectable Dutch ancestors. Both are irreproachable liquors, and rum deserves a better reputation; but pure, cold, transparent spring or well water, fresh from its bubbling fountain, or drawn from the cold recesses of its deep receptacle, has always been very attractive to me, and for washing purposes it has no equal. The prospect, therefore, of doing without water was unpleasant. Cows, and horses, and pigs have not learned to appreciate strong drinks; they prefer the native element; and to draw for half a mile from the nearest good pump as much as a cow and a horse can swallow would require pretty nearly the entire time of the latter.

In the midst of our troubles, the rope broke—not the golden cord, fortunately, of any member of the household, but the cord that was fastened to the pail. Here was a dilemma! To fish up a bucket out of forty feet of darkness was difficult; to use another pail till the first was removed was impossible. I began to think it would be necessary to dig a new well, when I was informed that a man could climb down the present one. This seemed to me a feat worthy of Hanlon; but I was prepared for the last extremities, even death itself—provided it was not my own—and simply said, "Let him do it," as though seeing men cling to a slippery wall of stones, like a fly on a pane of glass, had been the commonest experience of my life. How he managed I did not care to see; but that he did go to the bottom was proved by what he brought up, which was, not the pail, but—a dead cat!

Cats are a singular and unreliable race; they never possess the intelligence of dogs, and are given to strange vagaries. They roam about continually, and wander no one knows whither; but what should take a cat to the bottom of my well I can not understand. They are graceful creatures, and old maids and little children think them handsome; but, after they have been in water for three weeks, and become

A WELL. 93

much puffed up with their position, they are not handsome. Still, I was very glad to see that cat.

The well-water visibly improved, and the pump was finally completed. To be sure, the maker could not spare time to put it up, but other men were readily engaged, and one evening, on my return from the city, I found it duly installed in its place, looking very attractive. It was a neat and appropriate pump, and, remembering the inconveniences and dangers of drawing water with a pail, I joyfully seized the handle and commenced to pump. I worked away right manfully for a few moments, but did not manage to bring up any water. When I stopped for an instant, a long sigh seemed to express the thing's regret that it could not accommodate me, or the sufferings to which my exertions put it. I recommenced, and appeared to gain for a little distance, to judge by the effort required, but at a certain point success deserted me; the pump evidently was not equal to the occasion. I worked away on that hot August afternoon till the perspiration ran freely, if the water did not; and, when entirely convinced, if not satisfied, I indulged in as little strong language as the circumstances would admit, and sent for the pump-maker.

His bill had not been paid, and he came at once. When informed of the difficulty, he seized the pump-handle with amusing alacrity, but a few strokes changed his confidence to doubt. When he paused, the same appalling sigh that had greeted me announced a similar result, and I smiled amid my misery to see his manner change as he recommenced. After two or three attempts, he stopped suddenly and inquired,

"How deep is your well?"

A WELL. 95

He was not going to get off by any subterfuge if I could help it, so I answered promptly,

"Never mind that; the well is deep enough."

"But what is the depth? It is essential to know."

"Don't worry yourself about that now; fix your pump first," was the ready response.

"I can not do so till I know the depth of the well."

"Well, then, if you are so anxious to be informed, it is forty-five feet deep—deep enough, in all conscience."

"That is the trouble, of course; the pump won't suck."

"Of course it is, that is plain enough; and I expect you to give me one that will suck."

"But how can I?"

"That is your affair, not mine," beginning to be put out at the coolness of the fellow. "I want a pump that will suck!"

"Why," he replied, "don't you know that no pump will draw at over thirty feet?"

Suddenly the remembrance of school-days and their instruction came back to me; a vacuum and its properties, the weight of a column of air, and all that, returned to my mind after a long absence. I recalled the rule of fifteen pounds to a square inch, the power of suction—which for many years I had only tested with a straw and a julep—and the comparative specific gravity of water. Early education is a good thing, and the natural sciences are almost as practical as the learned classics. Without a remark, I left that pump-maker and his pump, and retired to the cool privacy of my neighboring dwelling. A wooden pump with a long rod is in my well, and it not only sucks, but lifts; the water is very fine.

CHAPTER VI.

A KITCHEN GARDEN.

TO the full enjoyment of a country house, there are few things more conducive than a large, well-filled kitchen garden. The farmers generally, with a wrong-headedness that is incomprehensible, neglect one of the most important sources of supply for the table; they devote themselves to the heavy crops—the staples of agriculture—that are scattered through the fields, and overlook the vast additional amount of food that may be concentrated in an acre. They condemn themselves to the everlasting routine of bread, potatoes, and salt meat, forgetting that the labor of a few hours occasionally of themselves or their children in the garden would furnish an agreeable, healthy, and nutritive variety of edibles. This, being a matter of dollars and cents as well as health, merited the closest attention from so practical a person as myself, and was taken in hand promptly, and the account of my success carries me back a little in matter of time.

It was late in April when the contract was closed for the building of the country house, and it was essential to prepare and plant the kitchen garden immediately. My ideas on the subject were vague. I knew what I wanted, but had not an accurate conception how those wants were to be converted into realities. I must have a choice, yet ample supply. Fresh asparagus is so delicate, fresh peas so tender, fresh lettuce so crisp, cauliflower so immaculate, cabbages so rich, beets so racy, and every other vegetable so much better when just pulled. There should be a plenteous variety, from the humble radish up to the aristocratic egg-plant—through all the range of carrots, turnips, celery, spinach, and cucumbers—every thing that creeps, climbs, or stands—but, above all, must there be a grand, deep, rich bed of asparagus, with heads as big as your thumb. The fruits, too, should not be forgotten: blackberries, gooseberries, raspberries, and especially strawberries; pears, plums, and apples—dwarfs and standards; currants, grapes, and quinces; the numberless productions of the earth that wise men eat before breakfast or after dinner. With these numerous necessaries, it was apparent that the planting must be done at once if it was to produce a satisfactory result this year.

But, before striking a spade, it was necessary to lay

A KITCHEN GARDEN.

out the ground, and here, although the undertaking was different from planning a house, my natural abilities stood me in good stead. After much study, the plot was divided into beds of about five feet width, so that the plants could be plucked without treading on them; I laid out broad walks at right angles to one another, like grand avenues, to be shaded by the future pear and apple trees, and in my mind determined to cover them with pure, white, salt-water pebbles. I left a narrow border along the outer edge for currant and raspberry bushes, marked places for the fruit-trees every fifteen feet, and devoted one bed to strawberries, another to tomatoes, a third to sweet corn, and so on. I noticed that there seemed to be about as much walk as bed, but this I had been accustomed to in flower gardens in the city, and thought produced a pleasing effect.

Before these dispositions were determined on, the grass had grown considerably, the spring being early, and to get rid of it, as "Bridgeman's Assistant," which, with "Ten Acres Enough," was my constant companion, contained no directions to meet the case, the advice of Weeville was called for. He said the land must be plowed, harrowed, and well dug over, and asked where the kitchen garden was to be placed. It was with no little satisfaction that I produced my plans, anticipating his surprise and pleasure, and laid them proudly before him. He gazed a moment, and exclaimed, "What is all this?" Not a little amused with his perplexity, I explained the design, and pointed out its advantages. He kept his eyes on it in a dazed sort of way, and then blurted out, "You have twice as much walk as you have bed."

"Not quite—not quite," I responded; "but still that is quite a feature; they will be attractive, covered with white gravel."

"White gravel! What is that for?" he exclaimed. "Nonsense; your walks will be overrun with weeds, and you will have enough to do to keep them out of your beds. I'll fix your garden for you, now I know where you want it."

Before I could protest, he rushed away, taking my plans with him, as though they were of no value whatever, with that wretched conceit which characterizes your practical man, not even waiting to hear a full explanation of my views, and evidently not appreciating them. He set his men to work next day without so much as consulting me.

Leaving Weeville's men hard at work with plow and harrow over the practical portion of the undertaking, I set to work with "Bridgeman's Assistant," and soon learned how to trench and make drills—

which, to my great astonishment, proved not to be holes—and became acquainted with the uses of the various garden implements. The quality and nature of the soil was quite a puzzle; but, as it had been ascertained by sinking the well that the upper six feet was a stiff, clayey substance, and beneath there was a pure stratum of sand, there could be little doubt but it must be a loam, which is described as a mixture of clay and sand. It was a fine, strong yellow, and my general impression was that loam is dark; but of its depth there could be no question, as the well-diggers went down forty-five feet before they reached water, and encountered no rock whatever.

There were many surprising statements in "Bridgeman's Assistant." It would seem natural that seeds, especially of radishes, beets, or carrots, should be planted at least a foot deep, so that the root might be long; but the author insisted that they should be covered with only two inches of earth. Unfortunately, however, as my investigations proceeded, some pleasing illusions were dissipated; one vegetable after another had to be given up, for the entire kingdom seemed to be governed by the most absurd laws; and when it was ascertained that strawberries would not bear the first season, and that asparagus might produce heads in the course of three years, I was in despair. Weeville, however, who confirmed these doleful discoveries, came to my rescue by inquiring in an enthusiastic way whether I had ever eaten a Daniel O'Rourke pea. I replied that doubtless I had, as I paid the highest price in market. .

"Oh, pshaw!" he answered, "they are never sol 1 in market; wait till you eat a Daniel O'Rourke pea, and then you can say you know what peas are. There are plenty of vegetables that you will be in time to plant; the ground is plowed and harrowed, and the Irishman is digging out the sods. A hard time he is having of it; the grass got up too high, and he has to break them up and shake each one out with a pitchfork. No person should live in the country without a garden; mine is the greatest comfort I have, and saves nearly half the expense of living."

So, it being clearly an economy, my investigations were pursued diligently. A long list of the best vegetables still attainable was selected, consisting of early Mohawk and Lima beans, blood turnip-rooted beets, long orange carrots, long green cucumbers, sweet corn, large green-head lettuce, silver-skinned onions, Dutch parsnips, and Daniel O'Rourke peas, and purchased at the seed-store for the moderate sum of four dollars and fifty cents, according to the particular entry made in my memorandum-book at the time. The necessary tools, such as wheel-barrows, spades, hoes, drills, cultivators, etc., were added, but the charge for these seems to have been omitted; and when Weeville reported that the first planting—two rows of Daniel O'Rourke peas—had been completed, I invited a couple of friends to ride over on horseback to see my country place, for I was still living in the city. The house was then in its foundation state, but the garden would be well worth a visit.

It is a beautiful ride to Flushing. An intelligent man, named Jackson, has built an excellent turnpike —almost the only one in our country—and, with justifiable pride, has called it after himself. The scenery is diversified with hill and dale, with fertile fields and dense woods, and, before reaching the village, the highway skirts the bay, and presents a clear view for some distance up the Sound. We clattered along past the bridge and through the village out to the five-acre plot. There it lay, bare and charming, without a fence, almost without a tree; the house scattered in every direction; the foundation going up and the well going down; heaps of sand collected here and there, and a platform for mixing mortar directly where the flowers ought to be; but where was the garden? We rode in every direction, and a last made out that a little bare spot which we had been over, forward and back, several times, and which was about twelve feet long by three wide, must be it. We did not dismount, but, consoling ourselves with the idea that the earth had been well stirred with our horses' hoofs—for stirring the earth is essential to a productive condition, as Bridgeman says—we returned to the city.

Next day Weeville went to oversee the Irishman, who was hard at work struggling to subdue the sods on another twelve feet by three, and was surprised to find many of the peas out of the ground. He took a hoe and replanted them, treading them down so as to keep them under for the future; and, having done this with a dozen or more, turned to Patrick, and told him that he must be more careful hereafter, and must cover the peas well with earth.

"Sure and I am sorely puzzled, sir," replied Patrick; "I have been all the morning poking the pays back under the earth. I've been thinking there must have been somebody over it, for they were all out of the ground intirely."

Considering that three horses had been trampling back and forth over the bed the night before, Patrick was about right. But he had other difficulties to contend with more formidable than horses' hoofs.

The sod was strong, not having been disturbed for years, and it was many days before there was any thing resembling regular beds. In time, however, the peas appeared above ground; egg-plants were transplanted; beans crept up, and demanded poles to climb on; queer-looking, weedy affairs, that Weeville designated cauliflowers or tomatoes, as he pleased, made themselves conspicuous, and the success of the undertaking seemed assured — when one morning Pat rushed up to Weeville's place, and, with staring eyes, announced that the cows had grazed off all the peas.

Any animal that entered that plot of ground appeared instinctively to know where the garden was, although better-endowed creatures might have trouble to find it, and either wanted to rest or pasture there, or at least to run over it. But when they proceeded to graze on the peas, it became serious, and upon Pat's announcing, the following week, that they had been at it again, Weeville called upon me to say that there must be a fence round the lot, or he would not answer for the garden. Pat was set to work at once building fence.

Since the days of the Tower of Babel, when the world was divided up into tribes, the nations have been distinguished by peculiar aptitudes. The English nation has a gift for building pirate ships, the French for fashioning new dresses, the Chinese for growing pig-tails and cutting off heads, the Russians for eating candles, the Turks for stealing wives, the Americans for doing a little of every thing, and the Irish for digging holes. Pat never could learn to use a saw or an axe, or even to drive a nail without splitting the wood, but he could dig against the world. He proceeded at once to make the holes for the posts of the fence.

While he was thus occupied, however, the garden was neglected, and as he could not by any possibility keep the holes in a line, and consequently wasted much time, the weeds grew apace. It requires a great many boards to reach round five acres, and the holes for the posts had to be very numerous. The cows, having discovered the superior qualities of Daniel O'Rourke peas, paid them regular visits, and kept them well cropped, so that the garden fared badly. Pat dug so many holes, in consequence of making them either out of line or at an improper distance, that he might almost be said to have trenched the lot; and by the time he was through, and before the posts were all up, or the fence more than half finished, it was time to cut the grass.

This was a season of scarcity of labor. The high

prices had satisfied the working-men that their time was too valuable to waste on every menial kind of drudgery, and they were particular, not only in selecting their masters, but their employment; so that Pat had to be the main reliance, with the occasional aid of a half-grown boy, to take hold of all the "odd jobs" required by a country place. He not only planted the garden, and built the fence, and helped in the house, and dug in the well, but he must mow the grass and milk the cow. In fact, if there was any thing that nobody else could or would do, Pat was called upon.

The grass was very fine. A handsome flower, with rich yellow centre, surrounded by a single white row of radiating petals, called a daisy—the lovely flower celebrated so frequently in English poetry, and the apt simile for all that is virtuous and innocent—had grown to great luxuriance, proving the uncommon richness of the soil. Its stalk was a foot long, and the pretty floweret topped the grass, and by its vast numbers lent a uniform tone of color to the entire lot. There seemed to be almost as much daisy as there was grass, which was what the natives called "switch grass," and they were both knee-high. This crop was especially thick and heavy on the upper portion of the plot, as the carts and wagons had been in the habit, entirely regardless of the enormous damages they occasioned, of driving over the lower end, and the cattle of the neighborhood had grazed it pretty thoroughly. There was, consequently, only about an acre and a half left to mow, and Pat, with the aid of the boy, had that done in a day or two.

In my youthful days, often "of a summer day" I had "raked the meadow, sweet with hay," and consequently had learned the importance of sun in haymaking. Unfortunately, no sooner was the hay cut and scattered about than there came on the heaviest rain of the season; it was a veritable northeaster, and lasted four or five days. The barn, which was expected to hold the crop, existed as yet only in anticipation; and when the hay did finally dry, it had to be collected in a pile, which Weeville called a stack, and left to the mercy of the elements. However, the labor cost only about seven dollars, and I was offered seventeen dollars for the stack, so that there was a clear profit of ten dollars. This was so encouraging that I felt almost inclined to lay down the entire five acres in grass, until I remembered that if an acre and a half produced ten dollars, five acres would only yield about thirty-five dollars—hardly sufficient interest on property valued at ten thousand dollars.

When the hay was stacked, and one board nailed on the fence so that the cattle could no longer wander wheresoever they listed, a careful examination of the garden gave the following result: Weeds profuse and luxuriant; vegetables scarce and sickly; peas about six inches high, well cropped, without flowers or pods; tomato-plants small, and well shaded by the surrounding weeds; egg-plants entirely invisible, having probably gone back into the egg in disgust; bean-poles tall and vigorous, beans about one foot high, being nearly up with the neighboring grass, and apparently unable to climb any higher. The other garden-truck was not to be found, and it required great discernment to distinguish the garden from the residue of the five acres. Weeville said it was no matter, after all, as he could supply me with whatever I wanted from his garden, and that it was always cheaper to buy vegetables than to raise them!

My glorious anticipations had dwindled; asparagus, cabbages, beets, strawberries, raspberries, pears, and plums had been given up; and now the hope of peas, beans, tomatoes, lettuce, and egg-plants was to be destroyed. That garden on which I counted so greatly—which was to have furnished not merely cheap food for my family, but subject for exultation over city friends—had proved a failure. Daniel O'Rourke peas were not to be; crisp lettuce could not be dressed in that style of art upon which I pride myself, and handed exultingly round to friends after the woodcock and claret, as so much superior to the stale, insipid stuff purchased in the markets. Egg-plants, richest of vegetables, were not to be pressed upon the surfeited guest as coming from my garden. Beans had proved a delusion, and tomato-vines a snare. All my study of horticultural works was to be thrown away.

It is true, we had raised an egg-plant, but it was small—so small that we thought of sending it to the agricultural fair as a rare production: it measured one inch and a half in circumference. We also raised one tomato, but a careless wretch trod on it, and crushed it and our hopes together. There was a fine lot of wild radish, which my friends pronounced to be weeds, although I had hopes for a time that a few of them would become tame. I was disappointed, however: they covered the new beds, as fast as these were cleared and dug, with a luxuriant clothing of bright green, and their leaves were pretty and graceful, but their roots never would come to any thing worth mentioning. It is deeply to be regretted that Nature has so constituted plants and weeds respectively, that the former won't grow and the latter will. I did not eat a Daniel O'Rourke pea after all.

CHAPTER VII.

THE FLOWER GARDEN.

THE results of the effort to produce a kitchen garden out of the raw material of virgin sod was discussed in the last chapter. When it was well under way, and after Weeville had, in his authoritative manner, taken it off my hands, I turned my attention to the flower garden. Of this I determined to take entire charge. I had not studied Bridgeman for weeks, nor peered into seedsmen's windows, and examined the peculiarities of all the plants that fell in my way, for nothing. Weeville might superintend the coarse vegetables if he pleased, but the delicate and elegant parterre of flowers that already existed in my mind's eye was to be my credit and responsibility alone.

It was some time before I could induce the masons to remove the platform for mortar that they had, with instinctive stupidity, placed in the centre of what was to be my principal bed; but I got them off at last, although they grumbled somewhat at being compelled to carry their loads a considerably longer distance. I had already marked out the general plan on paper with that skill which has been occasionally referred to; the main idea was taken from a Chinese puzzle, and had no equal in the most complicated productions of the ablest masters of landscape gardening, ancient or modern.

It is well known that, according to the highest standard of the art, the great point in laying out a garden is to avoid the monotony of tame regularity; and in that line little more could be done. There were beds shaped like stars and ellipses, worms and circles, triangles and octagons; some were round on one side and flat on the other; some had big heads and little tails, and others diminished to nothing at each end; there were sinuosities and projections, sharp points and easy curves, imitation bays and promontories; large beds suddenly contracted, narrow ones expanded; what promised to be a long stretch was broken off unexpectedly, and there certainly was no danger of monotony. Amid these wound the paths in the most admired irregularity, never leading where one would naturally expect, and giving the mind a vivid impression of the labyrinth.

The arrangement of the beds on paper was not difficult, but to trace them on the natural sod was another matter. This could not be intrusted to a common workman; one, to whom the plan was shown, insisted upon mistaking the walks for beds, and even proposed some alterations, which he called improvements. Somehow, I never was very good at the practical part of a design. Moreover, the weather had been dry, for this point had been reached toward the close of one of the rainless terms that alternated with the floods of this particular season. The ground was hard, the sun was hot, and my experience with a shovel—spade my man called it—had been limited; but the difficulty had to be overcome, regardless of previous habits, and, grasping the shovel bravely, I set to work at once.

The centre bed was a circle, and, by driving a stake in the ground, and attaching to it a string, there was no difficulty in making a faint impression of the outline on the grass. This outline I deepened into a shallow furrow with my spade, although my arms and back ached, and my clothes were damp with perspiration before I had finished. The next figure, which was a star, was not so easy; and when it came to the worms, and the bays, and promontories, there bid fair to be far too little monotony. In fact, the figures would not take the shapes they assumed on paper, and the more they were worked at the worse they grew. If they were narrowed, they became immediately too long; if they were lengthened, they had to be widened; if one part was taken off, another portion immediately bulged out; bays were either too deep or too shallow, promontories either stretched entirely across the adjoining walk or disappeared utterly. The walks were continually being squeezed into a strait that would not by any possibility admit the passage of modern crinoline, or spread out into a sort of desert waste. The truth is, such vulgar trivialities as are implied in practical performance are not suited to the intellectual mind. After working the plan several weeks, nearly killing myself, and sadly confusing the man I had hired for this express matter, I concluded to let him finish it alone. It is a matter of pride, however, that, in spite of some sad blunders through his ignorance, it still bears palpable traces of the original design, and entirely avoids the fatal fault of monotony.

While the man was completing the physical part, there was an excellent opportunity to select the best flowers that were to be procured. The study of botany is not a branch of the legal profession, nor even included in the limits of a classical education; but, fortunately, there is no necessity for knowing scientifically why the rose is red and the lily white provided one has the innate appreciation to enjoy the beauty of each. Perhaps it is desirable to be able to distinguish the plants when not in flower, but that is not absolutely necessary provided " Bridgeman" is always at hand.

The amount of information in this work is as inexhaustible as it is surprising. Under the author's manipulation, plants assume a fresh nature and exhibit new attractions; the most vulgar flower comes back decked in an aristocratic dress, and endowed with a name that is absolutely imposing. The common hollyhock—that vulgar, base, staring, and offensive flower—is suddenly converted into the delicate and refined althea; the larkspur becomes a delphinium; the old-fashioned Johnny-jump-up, a viola grandiflora; the commonplace poppy, a papaver; and the gaudy sunflower is transformed into the magnificent helianthus. The human mind is hardly prepared to accept gomphrenas for batchelors' buttons, and revolts from the association of the suggestive mirabilis with the commonplace four o'clocks. The kingdom of flowers, as it is usually called, becomes a model republic; the low and ignorant are elevated; the humble dweller in the hedge-row is raised to a place beside the tender production of the greenhouse; and the refined habitué of the ballroom is found to be twin sister to the wild inhabitant of the open field or native forest.

After some thought and careful consultation with the price-lists of all the seed-stores in the city, lest the utmost advantage should not be taken of the market, a list including the following principal varieties was selected: roses, pinks, carnations, lilies, fleur-de-lys, jasmines, peonies, verbenas, daisies, fuchsias, heliotropes, tulips, dahlias, crocuses, tube-roses, forget-me-nots, jonquils, wall-flowers, gillyflowers, mignonnette, fox-gloves, and china-asters. There were many others, but this selection is sufficient to show that the garden was to be well stocked. It is to be regretted that midsummer is not the most appropriate time to plant flowers, and that many of them require to be set out in earliest spring, or even the year before they are expected to blossom. Drought is especially unfavorable to the sowing of seeds or transplanting of roots, and the drought that had already begun to distinguish this midsummer positively forbade immediate action.

It is my impression that in early youth I remember reading of an ancient Roman who, having lost a valuable ring overboard at sea, subsequently caught the fish that had swallowed the ring. On recovering his property, he raised his eyes toward heaven, wondering what terrible calamity the gods had in store for him to equalize such good fortune. If there is no such story there ought to be, for nature is certainly made up of compensations. If a woman is rich she is rarely handsome; if a man is handsome he is not apt to be wise; if we are extremely fortunate we may expect a reverse; one misfortune wards off another; if we lose a leg in battle we are likely to save our head; the old motto says, "Lucky in love, unlucky in play;" and if it rains in spring, it is apt to be dry weather in summer. It had rained all through the spring as though the flood-gates of heaven never were to be closed, but when they were finally shut down they fitted so well that scarcely a drop trickled through the cracks. May was a deluge; July was a drought. All authorities coincide in holding that seeds must be planted before or immediately after a rain, but they give no directions how to produce a rain if it does not come naturally. It was in vain that I waited for even a shower—in vain that I scanned the sky at sunrise or sunset, watched the wind, or consulted the weather-wise. Clouds ceased to be the harbingers of rain; a threatening sunset only insured a cloudless morrow; an easterly wind was positive evidence of clear weather, and the sky was as blue as my feelings.

The time for planting one species after another of seed or root passed by. July came and went, August arrived and was slipping by, the list of seeds was fearfully reduced, when at last clouds covered the sky and rain began to fall. It is unnecessary to say that all such seeds as might by any possibility germinate so late in the season were, in spite of the pattering drops, planted ere the storm had fairly begun. Bridgeman's instructions had been learned by heart, and each kind was set out in a circle, while a stick with the empty bag, marked with the name, was stuck up in the centre. The trough in which they were planted was dug about two inches deep, and filled with manure, to insure vigorous growth. Two inches is deeper than was authorized, but it seemed desirable that the plants should take a deep root. Hardly were the seeds planted ere the rain stopped, the clouds broke, and the sun came out hotter than ever. For three weeks that sun never ceased to blaze except when it went to bed—for three weeks not another cloud appeared or drop of rain fell.

Tending a garden is a pleasant occupation, but when the only thing to be done is to water, every morning and evening, a spot of bare earth where seeds are supposed to be, it is monotonous. Some puppies that were kept by a neighbor, and which were forever trampling over my premises, chewed up and pulled out the sticks, and the location of the future plants became somewhat indefinite; and when Weeville asked me one day how my garden was getting on, I answered evasively,

"Finely, so far as I can see."

My conscience permitted me to presume all was going on right underground, although nothing had yet come to the surface. Not satisfied, however, he wanted to know exactly how I had set out the seeds; and when he was told they were planted two inches deep in a rich bed of manure, he burst forth,

"Why, you must have burnt them all up; plants want earth as much as manure. And if you buried them two inches deep, you dug their grave; not one will ever come up."

This coarse confidence on Weeville's part was not pleasant. I knew plants—thistles especially—would grow in manure, for my beds were full of them, and they appeared to do best when covered over and surrounded with the strongest lumps; but my mind had troubled me a little about the depth at which the seeds were planted; so, when he was gone, I took the first good opportunity to rake off about two inches of the earth.

It rained at last; vegetation started in every direction except where I supposed my seeds were; weeds spread over the beds, came up in the walks, and exhibited great luxuriance. I watched my garden anxiously, visiting it early and late; dreadful were my doubts and fears; but at last a circle of beautiful delicate green began to show itself, not exactly in the place I expected, but not far off. My delight was unbounded. I watched that circle like a mother would watch a sick child. I hung over it and tended it with most assiduous care. If the sun shone two days in succession, I watered it; if it rained too hard, I sheltered it. My triumph over Weeville was to be complete; it is true that only one out of the numerous varieties that were planted had appeared, but it would not be necessary to refer to the others.

That green circle grew slowly. The tiny leaves, in spite of the great care bestowed upon them, seemed to be feeble; their thin, pale stalks were hardly able to support their weight; the slightest rain threatened to wash them away, and a few hours of sunlight to scorch them up. I nursed them carefully through their infantile diseases; and when they were fairly past danger and presented a circle of unbroken green, I invited Weeville out to inspect my garden.

"Bare enough," he said sarcastically, as he passed

down the main path; "plenty of walks and weeds, but no flowers this year."

"Wait till you see," was my triumphant answer.

"I can see pretty well now," he replied; "there is certainly nothing to obstruct the view. I have a fine prospect of muddy walks and absurdly-shaped beds. You will learn to be practical before you are through. Another year or two will take the city nonsense out of you, and teach you some valuable lessons."

He was going on with his egotistical homilies, when I stopped him in front of my infant plants.

"Look at that!" I said, exultingly, grasping his arm and facing him toward the bed.

"Look at what?" he repeated, staring stupidly about.

"At those plants. Are they not promising? I intend to separate and transplant them: there will be abundance to stock half my garden. Rather better than raising egg-plants, eh? We city boys know a few things, after all. What do you think of those little beauties?"

"What on earth—or, more properly speaking, in the earth—are you talking about? I don't see any plants, or beauties either."

"Not see any plants!" I replied, laughing at his ignorance. "Perhaps you can not tell plants when

F

you do see them: you must study Bridgeman. These, sir, are the beautiful columbine *aquilegia formosa*, the most lovely ornaments of the refined and elegant parterre."

I did not know what they were, as the stick was gone; but this was the only name I could recall at the moment.

"May I ask," he replied, solemnly, "whether you are joking or crazy? If the former, it is too damp here to make it worth while to continue the entertainment; if the latter, the lunatic asylum is close by. What is it you are talking about?"

"Why, those *aquilegia formosas*, that beautiful circlet of exquisite green that I planted a month ago, and which assiduous care has finally brought to its present vigorous condition," I rejoined, smiling proudly, although my mind somewhat misgave me as to the vigorous health; "that fertile hot-bed of fragrant beauty, that will furnish the groundwork, with skillful increase, for my entire garden."

"What!" he demanded, in a surprised tone; "is that what you are talking of?"

"Yes," I replied, a little confused, but confident still.

"That your beautiful circlet of exquisite green which is to fecundate your entire garden!" At this point he commenced laughing, and, between shouts of merriment and the half-intelligible repetition of "exquisite green," it was ten minutes before he became comprehensible. "Why, that circlet of exquisite green—" here he burst out again till he nearly choked—"exquisite green is nothing but a lot of wild carrots, that you have watered till you have washed all the life out of them."

Alas! this turned out to be true. What became of my seeds I never discovered; whether they were drowned out, or burnt up, or raked away, is hard to tell; certain it is that they have not come up to the present time. But the greatest mystery is, why should wild carrots grow in a circle merely to arouse hopes that were to be blasted?

CHAPTER VIII.

POULTRY.

I HAVE a respect for chickens. The hens have the finest qualities of the most exemplary mothers; the cocks possess many of the characteristics, in courage and devotion to "the sex," of the cavaliers of olden time. Behold the anxious matron ruffling her feathers and expanding her wings in threatening defiance of the approaching stranger, or gathering the little ones under her breast, and exposing her own person to the swooping hawk. Observe the fierce-eyed rooster guarding his mates with zealous care, ever ready to meet in deadly conflict the rival or intruder, but invariably calling his wives to accept any unusual luxury of fat grub or dainty bug. To be sure, they rise early, which the uncultivated regard as a virtue, and make much noise when they wake, crowing at most unseasonable hours; but as for the absurd charges that the prejudiced author of "Ten Acres Enough" brings against them in wholesale condemnation, these are not worth answering.

What if they do scratch in the garden, it was clear that they could not damage mine; and do they not also catch the early worm that destroys the crop? Besides, chickens are good gastronomically, and eggs undeniable. They pick up most of their own food, and consequently are economical, and this, with so careful a calculator as myself, was sufficient. Their increase is vast, and the profit upon them immense. If every hen should only raise five broods yearly of ten each, and there were ten hens to start with, at the end of two years they would number three hundred and forty-four thousand seven hundred and sixty, after the superfluous roosters were sold; and then, supposing the extra eggs to have paid for their keeping, and the produce to be worth only a dollar and a half a pair, there would be a clear profit of $258,520. Allowing for occasional deaths, this sum might be stated in round numbers at a quarter of a million, which would be a liberal increase from ten hens. Of course, I did not expect to do so well as this, but merely mention what might be done with good luck and forcing.

Chickens had become very scarce about the time I wanted to purchase. Whether hens had given up laying eggs or raising young was not clear, but every old woman in the neighborhood to whom application was made informed me that chickens were scarce and high, and that she only let me have them as a special favor. Moreover, the breed of chickens kept at Flushing is rare and valuable; they were either Shanghais, or Dorkings, or Black Spanish, or something else extremely precious and desirable, and none of them were worth less than five dollars a pair. They were young and small, not yet exhibiting these remarkable attractions; but, as one old woman observed when I suggested this circumstance, "Sure you wouldn't expect a little chicken to be a full-grown hen the moment it comes out of the shell." This was so clearly reasonable that I made no farther objection, but purchased twenty pair of the best to be had. A coop was built, and the chickens turned in, Patrick remarking, in the process,

"Indade, they were the smallest lot that iver he saw."

I explained that they would grow; but he shook his head, and seemed to doubt it, and immediately proceeded to fill the smallest crevices in the coop, lest they should creep through.

Patrick fed and I watched these chickens faithfully. They were rather unhappy-looking things at the start, and as their principal amusement seemed to be plucking one another's feathers out at mealtime, their appearance did not improve. In a few days I observed that they had a strange way of opening their mouths, as though they were sleepy; but, as they went to bed at early candlelight, and slept, with little intermission, except for the occasional recreation of pushing each other off the perches, till sunrise, it seemed hardly possible, in spite of their early rising, that they suffered for loss of sleep. If they did happen to need more rest, no ready way suggested itself of supplying the deficiency—unless they attended to it themselves, which there was nothing to prevent—as I was not acquainted with an appropriate lullaby. So they were left to their own devices. Their yawning became infectious—as with human beings, when one gapes his companions will follow suit—until at last one, that seemed to desire to outdo the others or make up permanently for her lost time, "slept the sleep that knows no waking." This was bringing matters to a serious issue; and when two more were found on a subsequent morning stark and stiff, Weeville was sent for in all haste. He arrived in a short time with his usual cheery manner, and inquired "What was the matter now?" as though nothing ever went wrong with him, and as though he could put right every thing that went wrong with others. He was shown to the coop, where thirty-seven chickens were busily engaged opening their mouths every few seconds, as though they had taken into their throats a very large-sized grain of corn, and were unable to swallow it. It was an appalling sight. There was an earnestness and solemnity about their actions that removed all ludicrousness, and, with a painful feeling of despair, I asked what could be the matter with them.

"Why, they've got the gaps," Weeville answered at once.

If there is any thing unpleasant, it is to have a friend, whose advice you have asked on a serious matter—a matter in which your feelings are interested, if not otherwise very important—take advantage of the opportunity to indulge his wit. A joke is never a joke when uttered at the expense of a friend, or of the creatures, human or animal, for which that friend has an affection. The only way to punish such ill-timed pleasantry is to appear not to have felt it, and I responded carelessly, although internally indignant,

"You might better say they had the yawns. But, seriously, what is the matter with them?"

"I say they have the gaps; a whole black pepper—"

"Never mind carrying the joke any farther," I replied, firmly. "You may think it witty to say my chickens have the gaps, and I would laugh if possible; but, as three of them have died, it is no laughing matter. If you have nothing more useful to suggest, we will return to the house."

"I say they have the gaps; don't you know what that is? It is a regular disease, coming often from dampness, neglect, or inherent weakness—some people imagine there is a worm in the chicken's throat —and is cured by a change of diet, free exercise, and forcing whole black peppers down their throats. Let your chickens out of this miserable little hole where you have been suffocating them, and give them a change of diet, especially some worms or meat, and compel the worst to swallow a whole pepper every day or two. You may save a good many of them yet."

This was an exceedingly suggestive speech. My coop, which was some four feet square, was called a "hole;" my care and attention were termed "neglect;" and it was considered possible that I might save a "good many" of my pets. So I laughed at the idea, ridiculed his remedy, and told him there was danger that his "whole peppers" would keep them awake, and make them more "gapy" than

F 2

ever; but the moment he was gone, Patrick and I caught every chicken, and, in spite of struggles and cries, forced two whole peppers—for two were certainly better than one—down the throat of each, and turned them out of the coop.

They did not seem to be much improved by the operation, and went "gaping" round the premises in a miserable way, leaving one of their number dead here and another there, till they happened to attract the attention of my neighbor's pups. I have referred to these pups before. They were playful creatures; if there was any horrible and disgusting injury that they could, in a frolicsome mood, inflict upon me, they never missed the chance. They tore up the sticks that I set to mark my flowers; they scratched and dug in my strawberry bed, which I had succeeded in planting before the summer was over; they dragged in every direction my clothes that were laid out to bleach; they tormented my favorite cat; they appeared to think of nothing but plan deviltry against me, and do nothing but execute it. When the more flagrant of these wrongs had from time to time been inflicted, my neighbor called to apologize blandly and express his regrets, but never once proposed to kill the dreadful brutes.

The moment these pups saw my chickens they

started after them. The fluttering, squawking, and barking attracted my attention, and I gave chase to the pups. Away we went, chickens screeching with fear, the pups yelping with delight, and I storming with rage: "Come here! get out! go home! how dare you?"

If there had been one pup, I might have stood a chance; but, "being in doubt where to begin," I "both neglected." Each pounced on a chicken—of course, the largest and healthiest—and squeezed the breath out of them in a moment, and did not even give me the sweet satisfaction of revenge; but, having effected their object, and seeing me approach, stick in hand, bent on exemplary punishment, they each dropped their prey, and, darting through the neighboring fence, secured their retreat, or, as army men have it, "saved their bacon." This little amusement was renewed daily, and Patrick was continually on guard against a sortie of the enemy. But we became more skillful with practice, and a few well-directed blows and successful shots sent the enemy howling to the rear, and demoralized him greatly. Our chickens, however, had somewhat diminished in number; there were the killed, wounded, and missing, leaving quite a moderate residue. Moreover, there was a gentleman of Irish extraction living close by, who had kept chickens before I had; but it seemed to me that his flock increased as mine diminished, and I even thought that I recognized some of my "lost ones." It may be that they went there for safety, although, if any questions were asked, he could always explain how he came by that particular bird, and give its entire history, and the man's name that he bought it from.

When the pups were repressed and the gaps cured, and my remaining chickens—which were reduced to ten—were persuaded to stay at home, and when they had become large enough to give promise of future usefulness and eggs, Patrick was directed to prepare boxes for them to lay in. He filled these half full of soft hay, and deposited a white glass nest-egg, which cost twenty-five cents apiece, in each, and fastened them up in the most enticing locations. But the chickens did not seem to fancy the nests; in fact, they did not appear to turn their minds to laying at all, but were contented to "eat, drink, and be merry," without regard to their philoprogenitive duties. Patrick suggested that a little "mate" might bring them up to the required point, and, when that failed, said something about lime being required to make the shells; but I did not see the necessity for shells till we had the "filling" ready.

Certainly every inducement was offered those chickens to lay; they had abundant "feeds" of meal, and oats, and wheat, with "mate" twice a day, like an Irish servant-girl; they had the grazing of the entire "five acres," and most attractive boxes, but they did not seem to improve their opportunities. I had concluded that they were such a rare breed that they could not afford to overstock the market, and no longer wondered at their monstrous price, when Patrick rushed in to announce that the big Dominick—by which name he insisted upon calling a bird that had been sold to me as a Black Spanish of the most valuable kind—had a nest full of eggs.

"Sure and I jist found her out, the cunning baste; she stole her nest on me, and has it full of the purtiest eggs yez iver saw."

"Well, Patrick, that is a good sign; you must look round and find some more; they are all doubtless laying. Now go and bring me the eggs that you have found."

"Bring in the eggs, is it?"

"Certainly; it is too late in the year for setting."

"Sure, and how am I to do that?"

"Why, go and take them; you're not afraid of a hen?"

"But how am I to get there?"

"Walk, of course; what do you mean by talking to me in that way?"

"I don't mane any thing at all, at all, but I can't get the eggs unless your honor pulls down the barn. The old spalpeen has settled herself right under the middle of the flure, and meself spied her out through the cracks."

Sure enough, there she was. Utterly regardless of all the attractive boxes and imitation eggs, she had crawled away where only a rat could follow, and where a rat would, in the end, be sure to follow her, and had made her nest under the centre timber of the barn floor. There were two ways of reaching her—either by digging a tunnel such as our prisoners made at Libby, or by taking up the planks. As both of these modes would have cost somewhat more than the eggs were worth, even supposing she was a Black Spanish and not a Dominick—about which, I confess, I occasionally had some doubts—we never enjoyed more than a dim view through the dirty cracks of our "hidden treasures."

This, however, was rather encouraging; another hen might conclude to lay, and might select a more eligible situation. It was a difficult matter to get under the barn, and the next one might not be willing to take the trouble, even for the satisfaction of putting her master at defiance. But alas! the very next day Patrick waked me at daylight to announce that the fowls were "all dead entirely."

After a vain attempt to understand him, I hurried on my clothes, and, rushing to the coop where they were accustomed to roost, found it empty, and their murdered corpses scattered about in every direction. The small wounds, the unruffled feathers, the universal massacre, showed that a mink had done the deed. My chickens, my rare and valuable chickens, that were to have laid so many eggs and raised such countless posterity; the roosters, that were to have been fathers of a long line of famous descendants; the hens, that were to have been models of matronly propriety and parental self-sacrifice; my pets, that I had raised through so many dangers, that I had saved from one neighbor's flock and another neighbor's pups; my profits, that were to have put the author of "Ten Acres Enough" to silence, were cut off forever. Golden visions of eggs were destroyed; anticipations of tender spring broilers were disappointed; my quarter of a million of prospective profits—all were annihilated together by a mink.

We killed that mink. Like Oliver Twist, he returned for more, and met his fate. I had him stuffed, for one mink-skin is certainly a curious result from an investment of twenty pairs of chickens.

CHAPTER IX.

FALL WORK.

THE summer was pretty well over, and the various duties which accompany it accomplished after the manner already described; but there remained much to be performed as the cool weather approached. Not only is there the regular planting season in the spring, but Nature and Bridgeman permit some plants to be set out and seeds to be sown in the fall. September is the month for starting a strawberry-bed, and as my firm resolve was to have a grand plot of this best of small fruits, and as my first summer's success encouraged me to continue a country residence, Patrick was dispatched to the nearest nursery to engage two thousand plants, to be delivered on the breaking out of the first shower.

Here was the chance for me to make my fortune. The author of "Ten Acres Enough" lays it down as a maxim always to buy some new and hitherto unknown variety, that will bear the largest fruit in the greatest profusion, and insure not only a return for the fruit, but a good income by the sale of offshoots. So Patrick was directed to inform the nurseryman that I wanted a new kind, just discovered and superior to all that had preceded it. This request, though natural enough to any man who had studied the work referred to, must have seemed strange to the nurseryman, who was probably not literary, and who came back with Patrick to see about it.

He said he had several new varieties, but he was not entirely satisfied that they were better than the common ones. There was one, however, that promised well, called the Bonheur Seedling; but it had not been tested thoroughly. By-the-by, what excellent scholars all market gardeners are. Their ordinary language is Greek and Latin, and their nearest approach to that of common mortals, French. They overwhelm you with incomprehensible terms that early reminiscences assure you must be from one of the dead languages, and call every-day fruits *Duchesse d'Angoulême, Louise Bonne de Jersey, Belle Lucrative, Triomphe de Gand,* and so forth. I was not surprised, therefore, at hearing the new strawberry called "Bonheur Seedling," and rather took to the name as an omen of good luck. Without more ado, I ordered two thousand of the "Bonheur Seedling," while visions of enormous fruit and invaluable off-shoots floated before my mind. The man, anxious, no doubt, to keep the market to himself, suggested that perhaps I had better divide the order and take some of the ordinary kinds; but his object was too palpable to lead me from my purpose. If the Bonheur Seedlings were good for him to keep, they were better for me to plant, and so the order was not changed.

The drought of the summer continued, and, having parched the ground till it was as dry as an Irishman's throat the morning after election day, gave no signs of abating. September came in with a beautiful clear sky, remained with a beautiful clear sky, and went out with a beautiful clear sky. September is one of the finest months in the year, especially when the cloudless heavens permit the sun to send his warm beams to temper the cool breezes that begin to prevail, and, if a person has not a strawberry bed on his mind, no weather can be more enjoyable; but when agricultural purposes demand rain, even a cloudless September becomes tiresome. Patrick waited in daily expectation. He had managed to dig up the ground by the liberal use of a pickaxe and crowbar; but the sunshiny days were a trial to him.

FALL WORK.

"Shure I'm thinkin it's never going to rain agin," he said in despair, and the nurseryman was of the same opinion, for his patience gave out, and, without waiting for the actual falling of the precious drops, he took advantage of the first dark day, which did not arrive till the beginning of October, and sent the two thousand plants. Under these circumstances, and as Bridgeman says the beds may be made in October, if not finished before, there was nothing to be done but to soak the roots, thus trying to make them believe it was raining, as Patrick explained it, and set them out.

A strawberry is a thrifty plant; the only inconsiderateness it is guilty of is to fill its delicious pulpy fruit with nasty little crackling seeds; but give it the least chance, and it will grow. Ours were assiduously watered, and although, disgusted with the weather, some wilted away, others managed to "weather it," as our sailors say, and put forth a few feeble leaves in testimony of existence. By the end of October there were gaps in their regular ranks, but still the ranks were discernible, and the bed was an accomplished fact. I was not a little proud of this success. It is only necessary, in these cases, to take the thing in hand one's self, and I had kept the watering-pot in hand steadily.

Success in any undertaking in this life is a pleasant thing. The mere accomplishment of what we are aiming at, regardless of its importance, is a satisfaction, and a satisfaction that, so far in my country experience, I had not frequently enjoyed. There, however, was the bed: it was green with thriving beauty. To be sure, there were many weeds, but there were also a few "Bonheur Seedlings." Weeville made some disparaging remarks — something about my having a good bed in two or three years—

but I felt too complacent to mind him. So, when the cold began to increase, I had Patrick cover over my treasures carefully with plenty of straw, and possessed my soul in patience for the next spring.

The agriculture of modern days is very different from what it was in the times of our forefathers. Without going back to the days of Adam and Eve, when the vegetable kingdom managed itself, but after perspiration became a necessity of existence, the first gardening was rude, seeds were planted in the merest ignorance of all organic laws, and left to the fate that the earth and the waters held in store for them. Slowly, by innumerable failures, certain rules were learned, and fertilizers, rotation of crops, and suitable soils were dimly comprehended. In later days science has stepped in, and shed a flood of light on the subject. Now, before you plant a seed, you ask a chemist to analyze the soil, and ascertain exactly how much hydrogen, nitrogen, oxygen, phosphate of lime, and other ingredients with hard names, the dirt is composed of, and then you add whatever is deficient. One of the most beautiful inventions of science is liquid manure; not that it is beautiful in itself, for it certainly is not agreeable to the senses of smell or sight, and probably not to that of taste, but it does so admirably comply with all scientific requirements. The great object in applying a fertilizer is to so subdivide its particles as to enable the finer tissues of the roots to take it up by their almost invisible mouths. Not only is this done perfectly by dissolving the material to be applied, but water, the second great essential of vegetable life, is supplied at the same time. Upon this subject all the scientific books, including my favorites, "Ten Acres Enough" and "Bridgeman's Assistant," enter with an enthusiasm which is surprising to the novice. Of course I was a great admirer of the liquid theory, and resolved that my strawberries should not suffer from its want.

Nothing, however could be done till the following spring, and we must anticipate events to give the conclusion of the attempt. It was with some anxiety that I watched the removal of the straw covering the next April, and with no little relief did I observe that the "Bonheur Seedlings"—if they could be so called now that they had attained maturity — were still there; not quite so numerous, perhaps, as when they were covered up, and not by any means the original two thousand, but still to the number of several scores. The first thing to do was to give them a strong fertilizer, and that must be liquid. The drainings from the kitchen had been led into a sink, and, having fermented during winter, complied with all the requisites for this valuable nourishment. So deeply had I been impressed with the necessity of saving every thing that could supply plant-food, so entirely was I convinced of the force of scientific arguments, and the duty which every man owes to his country in aiding the fertility of her fields, that not a drop of the precious liquid had been wasted.

Patrick stared when he was told to water the plants with it, and murmured something about "its being too hot"—quite an Irish absurdity, considering it had been out all winter—but obeyed orders, and soon had a nice coating of what looked much like whitewash over the entire bed. After a day or two the "Bonheurs" were examined, and, not seeming very strong, were treated to a second watering; then, as they did not improve, fresh waterings were given them. In case of sickness science is our only resource, and, although Patrick ignorantly begged to have them left to themselves, the liquid fertilizer was applied steadily. It was given to them early and late; the weaker and paler they became, the more they had of it; once a day, twice a day, even three times a day, was the dose exhibited.

I am now satisfied that the " Bonheur Seedling" is not a success—it is not a sufficiently hardy plant for our climate. They may be good bearers—of this I can not speak—but they can not be called vigorous By the first of June the last had wilted away, in spite of steady waterings with the best liquid manure. My experience in this matter is of great value to the public; for, while I can advise no one to invest in "Bonheur Seedlings," I can thoroughly indorse the virtues of that universally praised and admirably scientific liquid fertilizer—the washings from the kitchen sink, and earnestly urge all young gardeners never to omit the use of it on their beds. If any thing can insure the success of the strawberry—even the "Bonheur Seedling"—it is this invaluable compost, and the directions for saving it contained in all agricultural works are well worth following, in spite of the trouble they entail. No one who uses it will fail to thank science for the benefits that it has conferred on agriculture. It is true that in my case it was not quite equal to the occasion, and I had to buy new plants and set them out in the spring; but I always regretted that the sink-water was exhausted ere this was done, for I felt sure that on any species but the feeble "Bonheur" so thoroughly scientific a fertilizer would have had a prodigious effect.

This very interesting matter has led us somewhat ahead of our story, and, although it seemed essential to give these valuable results of the application of science to strawberries, we must now return to our fall work. Next in importance to the strawberries was the asparagus-bed, and great were the preparations made for it. Bridgeman was consulted. He is somewhat obscure, and I did not practically understand some of his directions, especially the one which he lays down as of the first importance, that the plot of ground must be thoroughly "trenched." Of course, I was perfectly acquainted with the meaning of that word in its ordinary acceptation—it signifies to dig a ditch; but the exact purpose of a ditch in an asparagus-bed was not entirely apparent. It was not for drainage, for, as far as I could make out, the ditch was to be filled up again as soon as made; it was not merely as an ornament, or to separate these valuable plants from their baser and less aristocratic neighbors, but it had some occult purpose manifestly connected with a subtle and technical interpretation. An application to the last pictorial and unabridged "Worcester" did no good : there " trench" was made to mean a "pit, drain, or ditch." As "drain or ditch" were impossible, so "pit" seemed equally out of the question.

Not seeing any better way out of the dilemma, and the necessity to proceed being pressing, I put a bold

G

face upon the matter, and, in an indifferent sort of way, told Patrick to trench the necessary ground. To my great surprise and relief, he understood me, and I found it was not making a ditch round the plot, as I had suspected, but digging it well over and putting in manure. The roots of the asparagus were queer-looking things, without any green tops, reminding one of the frogs' legs seen in market strung on a stick, only that they have rather more legs than a frog. They were planted under my own supervision, and there we shall leave them until next spring, in the firm hope we shall see more of them.

The fruit-trees had to be set out in the fall, besides a forest of shade-trees; but, as this was done in October, after the cold weather had driven me to town, some painful mistakes arose in placing them; the fruit-trees generally found themselves where the shade-trees were to have been, and the smallest dwarfs usurped the locations of the tallest monarchs of the forest. This produced an irregular effect. There bid fair to be great thinness of foliage where we hoped for the densest shade, and the large trees were generally planted in such parts of the garden as required most sun; this, however, was not a serious matter, as they could be arranged in the ensuing fall, and it is not clear, after all, whether a little shade is

Fall Work. 147

not a good thing for plants in our extreme climate. This, with plowing and digging, closed our fall work, and in the next chapter we shall get a comparative statement of profit and loss, showing the manifold advantages of living in the country.

CHAPTER X.

PROFIT AND LOSS.

NOW that we have finished our first year's experience, and shown how readily a person can pass from the profession of a lawyer to that of an agriculturist, we come to the subject which, after all, is the great question of both city and country life, and which we have always kept so steadily in view— the question of profit and loss. The reader must bear in mind that I had great difficulties to contend with; no one had kindly set out fruit-trees for me, nor started my asparagus and strawberry beds, nor even laid out my garden. Moreover, the weather had been exceptionally hot and dry; for it does usually rain occasionally during the summer in our climate, and several accidents had happened that can hardly be expected to take place invariably. The profit, therefore, must be looked for, not in the merely vulgar, material sense, but somewhat in the sensations, thoughts, and experiences that were included in the results of the year's labor. To be sure, there was an indirect material gain : if I had gone to Saratoga or Newport, or had hired a summer residence elsewhere, $2000 or $3000 would hardly have covered the expense, even if I did not fall into the clutches of the "tiger ;" and if I had staid in the city, at the present price of mint juleps and sherry cobblers, and the present dusty condition of the public thoroughfares, I could hardly have got off for less. The pure air of Flushing supplied the place of both these excitements, while the deep interest of my agricultural pursuits kept my mind in a pleasant state of occupation.

The original outlay for house and grounds was, in round numbers, $15,000; my fruit-trees cost $145 50, which must be added to principal of investment, as it was not to be expected I should have to buy fruit-trees every year. The strawberry plants cost $20, and this should also be part of principal; but, as they all died, it may be that this must be yearly expense, at least for the first season. The asparagus plants cost $25, and we can hardly be able to tell where to place that item until next year shall determine what becomes of them. The baker's boy, who served me with bread, ran his cart against my gate-post, and put me to an expense of $35 for repairs; this clearly should be principal, as he could hardly be expected to renew the operation yearly; besides, he has been dismissed by his employer. My seeds cost $3 75, and, as they never came up, I fear they must go to annual expenditure. The bean-poles cost $2, and, if the neighboring boys do not steal them, that is an item of investment. The nest-eggs for the hens cost 75 cents, which, I have been informed, is more than they are worth; but that constitutes permanent capital. My furniture was badly damaged in being transported from the city to the country, and then from the country to the city; the legs of the chairs became somewhat displaced, and the upper drawer fell out of one bureau, that was laid face downward; but, as I am now suing the express-men for damages by reason of their negligence, it is hard to say whether this should be included; I have put my damages at $250, but, perhaps, for the purposes of this work, we might reduce them to $25. Dandy Jim cost $450, and ate about half as much in hay and oats, and smashed my wagon to such an extent that the repairs came to $50, and the wagon was nearly ruined. I paid $100 for the cow, and would not part with her for twice the money. The chickens cost $105, which item must go to annual expenditure, less the value of one mink skin. The pig cost $12, and grew finely, eating not only all the kitchen refuse, but a good feed of corn-meal and water three times a day; unfortunately, pork fell, and when he was killed he would only have produced $11 in market; but, as we intended to cure and eat him, he would have been fairly worth what we should have had to pay for salt pork by retail, had not an accident happened that will be described hereafter. The value of the premises was really greatly enhanced by their occupation and the improvements made on them, but the precise amount of such increase is too indefinite to be stated with the accuracy required by this work, consequently it is omitted altogether, the intention of the writer being to give only such items as may be fully relied on by any person intending to embark in a similar venture.

The account may be stated as follows:

INVESTMENT.—DEBIT.

Premises	$15,000 00
Fruit-trees	145 50
Shade-trees (mostly in wrong places)	107 00
Asparagus plants (doubtful)	25 00
Repairs to gate	35 00
Bean-poles	2 00
Dandy Jim	450 00
Cow	100 00
Nest-eggs	75
Total	$15,865 25

INVESTMENT.—CREDIT.

Premises worth	$15,000 00
Trees (besides improving the premises)	350 00
Asparagus-bed (if successful)	150 00
Bean-poles (if not stolen)	2 00
Dandy Jim (would be glad to take)	200 00
Cushy (would not sell her for)	200 00
Nest-egg (all but one lost)	05
Total	$15,902 05

The increased value in the trees is due to the fact that they have been standing some months, and are really worth so much more on one's place than crowded together in a nursery. A few may die—but it is not well to anticipate misfortunes—and the expense of replacing them will, in such case, fall into the annual account of the succeeding year.

YEARLY EXPENDITURE.

Interest on investment	$1050 00
Strawberry plants	20 00
Seeds	3 75
Damages to furniture	25 00
Repairs of wagon (yearly expenditure so long as Dandy Jim remains with me)	50 00
Chickens	105 00
Total	$1253 75

YEARLY PROCEEDS.

Expense of trip to Newport or Saratoga saved	$2000 00
Proceeds from suit against express-men	50 00
Costs, ditto	200 00
One mink skin	25
Total	$2250 25

The profits of my first year were not large, but sufficient to induce me to continue the experiment. There may be some few items of expense, such as neglect of business, which are omitted; but the amount is difficult to compute, and rather too remote, as we lawyers say, for the business might have been neglected in any event. The mink skin was taken at a bad season of the year for the fur; it is included among the annual receipts as an offset to the chickens, and in the confident expectation that if another mink were to do similar damage he would suffer the same fate. The clear profit may be set down at $1000 in round numbers, which was entirely satisfactory, considering the unusual difficulties that presented themselves, and which more experience and less drought would probably remove in succeeding years. It will be observed that the costs of suit are included, although the case is not yet tried; but as it is a question involving a long account of many items, and is brought by a lawyer, the judge will probably refer it to another lawyer, who will undoubtedly perceive the justice of the claim. The amount of both recovery and costs is rather understated, if any thing. This is a source of profit that could only be counted on by one of the profession; a non-professional would probably find it the other way; but, as the damages are charged, the receipts must go against them. The saving on the trip to Newport or Saratoga is fairly included, as none of my readers would expect me to pass the summer in town.

This was certainly, taken all in all, a flattering exhibit, as, with the charming and original author of "Ten Acres Enough," when he forgot to put any clothing on the backs of his wife and daughters, we must not confine our view merely to the humdrum matter of fact affairs of every-day life, but must look at the whole subject from a higher stand-point. Think of all the pleasures, intellectual and physical, of the change from the dull, dreary city streets to the lovely country roads—from the nasty Croton, running through its poisonous leaden pipes, and vulgarly penetrating into every room on every story, to the pure, sparkling well-water, so fresh and delicious (after the cat was removed), drawn from the deep well by pump or bucket. Think of going from the unhealthy atmosphere of overcrowded New York, where sickness of all kinds is on the look-out for its victims—where pestilence stalks in the noonday—to the invigorating air of Flushing, where a slight attack of chills and fever, if it does happen, is rather an agreeable variety. Think of escaping from the offensive over-supply of Fulton and Washington Markets, and the consequent difficulty in making selections for the daily returning dinner, and being every morning informed by the butcher-boy that you can have a beefsteak or mutton-chop, and nothing else, according as hairy or woolly cattle are cheapest. Think of all these advantages, apart from pecuniary considerations!

In a moral aspect, the advantage is equally striking. No late hours or evening dissipations at Flushing—no demoralizing club-life—no theatrical entertainments—no political meetings. Occasionally, perhaps, some exponent of the water-cure theory, some second-rate necromancer, some believer in spiritualism, or some devotee of cold water, gives a lecture at the town hall; but these can scarcely rise to the dangerous dignity of dissipations, and are agreeably somnolescent in their influence. Husbands are not apt to be led away by them into neglecting their wives, nor literary or professional men into deserting their books; while for the youth of either sex these attractions are not excessive. Once in a while there may be a public ball, but, as every one has been seeing every body else every day in every week for months, if not years, and as nothing but ice cream, cakes, and lemonade are served round, it is a mild species of orgy at worst.

But, to escape from moral considerations and to return to practical ones, it will be observed that the pig does not appear in the accounts; this is due to what may properly be called an accident, and can not be blamed to the writer. Piggy grew finely, and toward Christmas Patrick butchered him in artistic style, and brought him to the city. He must have weighed 220 lbs., although, not having scales sufficiently strong to sustain that weight, I can not be positive that he did not exceed it; but, unfortunately, the price of pork was then only five cents per pound, which would have brought him to eleven dollars, whereas we had paid twelve for him six months before, and put a goodly amount of corn, to say nothing of swill, into him besides. He was not for sale, however, being intended for the salting-kettle, and I proceeded to cut him up.

I was not skilled in the art of animal dissection, and the result would hardly have been approved by a scientific butcher. His back was particularly hard to split, especially with no better instrument than a heavy carving-knife, which was somewhat nicked in the operation, and it was very difficult to chop in the true line. Surgery not having been a part of my education, I found the disjointing of the limbs an intricate process. The shoulders and hams took

PROFIT AND LOSS. 157

odd shapes, unlike what I had been accustomed to seeing on table, and the flesh insisted upon looking more like gobs than the ordinary pieces. Still, Patrick was strong, and he pulled as I cut, and between us something was sure to give way, and I succeeded in separating the joints, and reducing him to a shape

that would go into the barrel, the abundant fat that I encountered in the process promising well for the quality of the future salt pork that he was to make.

Weeville had given me an accurate recipe for preparing the brine that was to cover him: it was to be composed of salt and water boiled, and strong enough to bear an egg, with a modicum of saltpetre. The hams and shoulders were to be rubbed well with brown sugar, with a view to their being smoked, and the brine was to be poured over the pork after the latter had been carefully packed in the barrel, and then a weight was to be laid on top.

These directions were very explicit, and it seemed impossible to make a mistake; but, unfortunately, Weeville forgot to mention that the brine must be allowed to cool before it is used. Being ignorant of this important particular, I poured the boiling pickle over the meat, which had been carefully disposed in the bottom of a huge hogshead, and calmly awaited the effect. Without entering into farther particulars on this painful subject, it is sufficient to say that we did not eat our own salt pork that year. It would undoubtedly have been remarkably fine, and far superior to any thing that is to be had in market, for it is my firm impression that that pig had eaten three or four times its weight in corn before it had consented to harden its flesh, which my scientific neighbors tell me is the object in feeding corn. I bore the disappointment as well as I could, but it is to be regretted that people are not more careful to be exact in their instructions; and, above all, when an error of this kind is committed and pointed out, they should not reply—as Weeville was inconsiderate enough to do, when I told him of his omission—"Well, I thought you knew enough for that."

This loss, being a mere accident, for which I was clearly no more to blame than if my pocket had been picked in the cars, or I had trod on a nail when surveying my garden and been compelled to pay doctor's bills, is not fairly chargeable to the account of country life. In fact, the loss took place in the city; for when the pig left the country he was manifestly worth eleven, if not twelve dollars, at market rates, and was even more valuable for home consumption. The loss was not my fault, nor the pig's fault, and Weeville says it was not his fault—and it certainly was not the fault of country life—so I have omitted it altogether from the statement.

I have been particular to be thus explicit and exact, and to keep every thing within bounds; for, knowing what numbers will be induced by these pages to follow my example, I wish to give them merely such views and facts as they can implicitly rely upon; and it is confidently believed that any other professional man can do as well as I did, or very nearly so, with any five acres he may select in the vicinity of Flushing, or in some other equally eligible locality, if any locality as eligible as that delightful and fashionable village can be found—a point about which, until my lots are sold, I shall continue to have very great doubts.

CHAPTER XI.

THE FLUSHING SKATING-POND—A DIGRESSION.

"WELL," said Weeville one day, during the ensuing winter, as he dropped into my quiet office in the city, where I try to forget the charms and allurements of the country, and devote myself to Coke, Blackstone, and Kent, "we have finally put our skating-pond in good hands. Last year there was much complaint because the snow was not cleared off, and the best days in the season were wasted from this neglect; but now we shall have no farther trouble. You know the ice-man, Willis, who supplies the residents with ice—he has taken hold of it. His services were engaged at considerable expense, because we all knew his long experience had made him thoroughly acquainted with the subject. He has had to do with ice ever since he was a boy; he has cut it, and packed it, and sold it, and can make it freeze if there is any freeze in it. During the mildest winters his supply has never failed; he is a remarkable man in that line. We have a splendid pond, nicely fenced in, and much superior to your Central Park affairs, where the boys jostle and upset you, or to the petty concerns got up as rinks, and occupying half a city block, where you can scarcely turn round. There is plenty of room on our lake, and the company is select. You are fond of skating. Why don't you make up a party and run out some day? All the best people go there, and you know how pretty our girls are in Flushing."

I hâd come to the city quite early, not being entirely satisfied, in my blind ignorance, that winters in the country, with snow or mud on the ground, the thermometer clinging to zero, and the wind having full sweep, were as pleasant as they are in New York, even when streets are impassable and sidewalks slippery. Nevertheless, I am devotedly fond of skating; not that I excel in the art; for, on the contrary, I can do little more than the simplest steps, and generally return from every expedition with bruised body and sore limbs. I keep on hoping that I shall improve, and make the most of the fresh air and exercise, although the fancy steps, and my efforts to disregard the simplest laws of equilibrium, bring me to grief. It is pleasant to skate, and pleasant to see others skate, especially of the female sex, with their cheeks aglow and their eyes sparkling, and with their neat dresses and dainty feet. On the Central Park the troublesome boys annoy me, and the private ponds are so filled with superior artists that I am ashamed to appear on them; skating is not only a fashionable recreation, but peculiarly a country pastime, where ponds abound, not having been filled up to make city lots; so I determined to take advantage of Weeville's suggestion.

Moreover, I am fond of the best people; I like good society. It is pleasant to mention that I met so and so, and imply that we are on intimate terms. Of course, all are equals in this country, and my family is exceedingly old, going back almost to the time of my grandfather. I have a right to consideration, but still one feels better to be among the best. Besides these two attractions, Weeville had intimated that the young ladies of the neighborhood frequented that favored pond; this was a still stronger inducement. Woman is pretty in every costume that fashion adopts; she is angelic in high bonnets and divine in flat hats; she is bewitching in tight skirts, and enrapturing in balloon crinoline; she is entrancing in short robes, and overwhelming in long trains; whether she wears feathers or ribbons, crape or colors, high necks or low necks, she is charming; but in a skating costume, with her dress high looped up, her red balmoral appearing below, and her dear little feet—seeming smaller from being strapped to skates—peeping out from under all, and occasionally exhibiting an ankle above, she becomes tenfold more enchanting. The exercise and cold air are splendid artists for painting her cheeks, and the swan is nowhere in comparison with her grace of motion. No place so abounds in the beautiful of their sex as Flushing. So I resolved that I would steal a day from pressing cares and labors, and collect a few friends to visit the skating pond.

The house had been finished and closed, and had been given in Patrick's charge; some furniture had been left there, and it was merely necessary to make a few arrangements to receive hospitably the guests who had been invited. Weeville was to bring me word when the ice was solid, so that we might start on the ensuing morning early. The thermometer was the subject of much interest for some days. It went down finally, and staid down resolutely; rumors circulated that the New York Rink was frozen, and skating had commenced there; next the public conveyances bore announcements that the opposition private pond was solid; and finally the red ball went up, and thousands rushed to the Central Park. Our party, too much on the *qui vive* for the superior attractions of Flushing to make engagements for any of those places, waited and waited for Weeville. After the rest of the skating world had been enjoying themselves for a week, he appeared at my office in a great state of hilarity.

"Ready at last," he shouted. "Willis wanted the ice to be solid; a careful man, that; no accidents while he is in charge. But last night fixed it. The ice is at least six inches thick, and to-morrow the whole town will be on hand. Nothing like starting right; put some one with brains at the head, and you are sure to go straight; twenty years' experience does not pass for nothing. I suppose you have been impatient, but remember we have no life-saving machines, and it is better to be on the sure side, if it is a little slower. Come in the early train to-morrow."

There was great excitement in warning and collecting our forces, and we did not get off as early as we hoped; but having at last managed to cross the river and reach the train—except a few couples that were left behind—we were soon at the Flushing dépôt.

Instead of having wagons ready to carry the party at once to the pond, as he had promised, Weeville received us alone. His usual hilarity was wanting, his air was sad, his manner disconsolate. As we crowded around him, he said slowly, "There is no skating."

"Ridiculous," was the answer, in a chorus of astonished voices; "there must be skating."

"Yes," said our precise associate, "I have a recording thermometer, and last night the mercury fell to fifteen."

"Your man is a little too cautious," I said; "there is such a thing as erring on the right side."

"Oh!" said the ladies, "if that's all, we are not afraid; are we, Mr. —— ?" each turning to her particular companion with a look that induced the latter to engage unanimously to answer for their safety.

"But there is no ice," again said Weeville, with a manner of most deplorable abasement.

"Now, how can that be?" demanded our precise man again; "water freezes at thirty-two."

"Why," burst forth the female chorus, "the Central Park has been frozen these two days."

"Well, Mr. Weeville," I then commenced, growing incensed at his stupidity, "if there was no ice, why did you tell me last evening that it was six inches thick?"

"So it was," he replied, still more drearily.

"Then, in Heaven's name, what has become of it?"

"Willis cut it all yesterday, and put it in his ice-houses," was the final reply. If he had fired a pistol among the party, my friend could not have surprised them more. "He says he wanted it to freeze smoother; but the pond is ruined for the season, as the little pieces and lumps that have broken off will remain and destroy the surface."

"What a shame!" cried the ladies. "The scoundrel!" growled the men. "Well, what can we do?" asked the former. "Let us go home," replied the latter. Vain were my imploring requests that they would at least visit my country seat—in company I speak of it as my country "place" or "seat"—that they might warm themselves after their journey, and satisfy the cravings of hunger and thirst. "All aboard!" yelled the conductor, for the Flushing trains make immediate return trips, like ferry-boats. My companions clambered up the steps and into the seats, and, in a moment more, were being whirled back to the city. I did not accompany them, but remained with Weeville, who, though far from lively, was probably a more pleasant associate for me just then.

In fact, on the question of skating the city seems to possess certain advantages. In the country snow keeps falling at odd and inconvenient times, and there are no enthusiastic individuals to shovel it off.

Hardly does the thermometer go down into the twenties, and succeed in congealing the surface and raising the expectations of the devotees of the "ringing steel," ere the clouds cover the sky, snow-flakes make their appearance, and settle down with some inches of soft impassability, winding up, probably, with a rain or "freeze," that leaves the entire surface of every pond an uninviting expanse of "humps and bumps," that bid defiance equally to high art and unskilled blundering. The ice-shaving machines, the snow-sweepers and the like, are confined to the metropolitan limits; and, although there is plenty of ice in the country, it is often hard to get at, even if there is not an "ice-man" to carry it away for other uses than skating.

CHAPTER XII.

THE SECOND YEAR.

WE now come to the second year. The house had been finished. It occupied a commanding position on the beautiful square that constituted my possessions, and, with the wind whistling through the innumerable ornaments that covered the edges of its high peaks, brought to mind its original seafaring owner. The land had been well plowed, at last, and was no longer impervious to spade and pick; the strawberries, whose untimely fate has already been described in anticipation, had been planted, and the asparagus-bed was in a promising state of preparation. Fruit-trees, and raspberry bushes, and the "great Lawton blackberry"—which, having originally been discovered by Mr. Seaton, was called by my intelligent fellow-farmers after Mr. Lawton, because both names ended with " ton"—were set out; my accounts for the year were made up, and I determined to go to Europe.

My trip was principally undertaken—apart from some business claims which importunate clients insisted on pressing upon me—to study the European mode of agriculture. With that view I spent most of my time in Paris, and went steadily to the Jardin des Plantes, Jardin d'Acclimitation, Jardin Mobille, Château de Vincennes, Château des Fleurs, the Lilac Festival, Bois des Boulogne, Parc Monceau, and all such places where there was a chance to learn any thing I did not know before. The information I acquired was very valuable, and if the reader perceives its effect in the future pages he need not be surprised.

This threw the garden pretty much upon Patrick's shoulders, and he bought me a new lot of forty chickens, two watch-dogs, and four cats—as the rats had almost taken possession of my house and barn, thinking, apparently, that it was built for their convenience—and put into the ground the most enormous quantity of manure. He seemed to have imbibed the scientific agriculturist's admiration for fertilizers, or else felt an interest in the welfare of his numerous friends and compatriots in the neighborhood who kept pigs and cattle, and raised what the books politely term compost. He spread seven hundred loads of it on my five acres, and when he was through there was not a load of compost to be had in Flushing for love—although I do not believe that ever bought a load of compost any where—or money.

Of course, I did not know exactly what seeds Patrick had put in, and if I asked him, during the spring, whether he had this or that vegetable, his answer always was, "Shure and he had lashings ov it;" but I feared he had a sneaking weakness for onions and cabbages. My first question on my return, which was after a flying visit of a few months, in which I had learned all that was essential, was about the success of the asparagus-bed.

"Faith, nothing has iver come up," was the heart-rending response. "There was a most beautiful pond of water standing on the spot all winter, and I consaited that the roots was rotted out intirely; so, as the bed was ilegantly manured, I jist put in a fine crop o' turnips, as I thought that would be the doin' ov it."

This was the end of my asparagus—a bed that requires three years to mature, and which could not be started till another fall; a bed that had been trenched and fertilized, and on which so much brain-work and back-work had been expended; a bed in which the roots ought to have slept comfortably and safely during their sleepy season. One or two spears struggled up through the second planting, but even they were feeble, and barely exhibited that delicate fringe that mature asparagus assumes by contrast to its earlier state. My disgust can be imagined—to plant asparagus and reap turnips, which I never eat, and yet have Patrick inform me that this was "the doing of it!" To have, in place of the most aristocratic and delicate of vegetables, the most vulgar and indigestible one; to have the favorite plant of refined gourmets supplanted by the food of cattle! I felt as though the only thing "done" was myself.

Although my return to farming was a little late in the season, I went to work in earnest, undismayed by this deplorable failure, planting every spot that Patrick had neglected, and, as his memory was not very accurate, occasionally putting a second sowing where he had already planted a different seed. I felt I must make the most of my ground in its present productive condition, and filled up every hole and corner. The weather was propitious, and every thing grew in grand style. The peas climbed up the bushes that were set round them and out over the top; the beans went to the summit of their poles, and then waved their heads round in the wind like measuring-worms on the end of a stick; and the squashes covered the ground with enormous leaves.

The first that came to bearing were our peas—

Daniel O'Rourkes, of course. They rather went to stalk, being some seven feet high—about twice their proper height, as laid down in agricultural works, and almost out of reach. There were not many pods, and Patrick said " he 'most broke his back laining up to reach 'em;" but the flavor fully justified Weeville's enthusiasm. Unfortunately, only two rows had been planted, and they furnished but a few meals—we had moved out of town early to enjoy the full benefit of our fresh vegetables—and our next planting consisted of a quantity of dwarf marrowfats. Now dwarf peas have some advantages; they are easy to plant and easier to take care of; they grow luxuriantly and bear abundantly; they are what farmers call a "sure crop," but as for eating them, that is another question. In a religious and penitential point of view they would be invaluable, as no amount of boiling would ever soften them. It is said they are a profitable crop, and good, when plowed under, to enrich the land. It would seem as though they were excellent in every way but on the table, and it so happened that it was just for this especial purpose that I wanted them. My land needed no farther enriching —Patrick's compost had done that effectually. Piety, of course, is desirable in its way, and penitence is necessary, but mine never ran in the pea line; and pilgrimages in tight boots was as much as ever I could endure and retain a pious frame of mind, without adding the torture of dwarf peas. Patrick, however, had great faith in dwarf peas, because they required no bushes, and had consequently planted little else, so that our taste of Daniel O'Rourkes was tantalizing. After the latter were gone we bought the peas for our table in the village, while I had the satisfaction of feeding Patrick the dry, tasteless "dwarfs" all summer, till he thought the "dwarf pays weren't good at all, at all."

Our next crop was squashes. We had the earliest squashes in all Flushing. Their broad leaves covered the ground and reached up like hands toward heaven; their insinuating runners spread in every direction; large yellow flowers, into which bumblebees retired for honey till they were out of sight, appeared innumerably, and at last the creamy, delicate fruit shone through the thick foliage. It was with no little exultation that I handed a fine large ripe one to Weeville, whose vines were not nearly so forward. I anticipated his surprise, and watched for its manifestation with interest. He, however, thanked me kindly, but said he never ate squashes. This was simply the effect of envy. He was indignant that his scholar should have been ahead of him, and pretended he was merely raising a few for the servants. The excuse was a palpable evasion, and I did not allow it to depress me, although I must confess that I do not eat squashes myself. Peas are fine, especially Daniel O'Rourkes, and except dwarfs; but squashes are a miserably watery vegetable, fit only to feed cattle, who will hardly eat them—except always when one raises them one's self, and has the earliest in the neighborhood, then they must be eaten with a relish, and I did my best to keep up appearances.

Our cucumbers were a marvel of success. The

water and musk melons did not do so well, although the squashes were placed on one side of them and the cucumbers on the other. Unfortunately, I do not eat cucumbers either. The onions succeeded admirably—almost too much so, for Patrick, as I had dreaded, had planted about an acre of them. I should have eaten these, but there is a popular prejudice against them, and I observed that after indulging in them, if I paid a visit, my lady friends did not care to hear me whisper sweet nothings into their ears. Our turnips and cabbages were immense, but it was never expected that any one but the servants and cattle would touch them. The cauliflowers and egg-plants did not do so well. Patrick made an effort to sell our surplus vegetables, but the market seemed to be supplied, or the price turned out very different from what we were in the habit of paying when we purchased. They mostly went to Cushy, Dandy Jim—who rather turned up his nose at them—and the pigs, of which Patrick had purchased an entire litter.

I am a great admirer of cauliflowers, with their creamy consistency and delicate flavor, and when July arrived, as ours evinced no desire to hold up their heads and "blossom like the rose," it was clear "something must be done, and that shortly."

Fresh application was made to the books, but the information there contained was not quite so full and satisfactory as had been expected. Much was said about cold frames, and housing young plants for the winter, but very little that seemed to meet the case in point. My plants did not want any housing over winter; they were to be eaten at once, if they would only come to the edible point. The sole difficulty was that they presented to the eye nothing that in the least resembled what one finds in market under the name of cauliflower—a delicious concentration of vegetable cream. There were leaves and stalks, but no flower, and what precisely the former were good for except to feed the cow, neither Patrick nor myself could exactly tell. He had a very vague idea of the cause of the difficulty, and all that the books seemed to suggest was a return to that most useful nourishment, the liquid fertilizer.

Our kitchen sink having been exhausted on the strawberries, this had to be manufactured from the refuse of the chicken coop. It was not a refined idea to pour such a filthy compound over so absorbent a substance—in fact, over any substance that was to be eaten—and the necessity of success alone forced me to it. But the plants were themselves evidently disgusted with such treatment, and only spread out their leaves like umbrellas to shield themselves from the offensive showers. We had a few heads, or what passed for heads; but they were leafy and rather tough—quite different from the white full heads sold in market—and we fancied tasted of their nourishment.

There seemed to be a spell on the garden; whatever we wanted failed, and had to be purchased in the village, and whatever was useless grew magnificently. One of our cucumbers measured two feet in length by one in circumference, and took the prize—a certificate merely—at the county fair; but, generally, our success was not in exact accordance with our taste. This, of course, was due to my unfortunate absence early in the season. It never does to leave such important matters to unlettered ignorance. How Adam ever made out to earn his bread in early days, without the aid of "Ten Acres Enough," and "Bridgeman's Assistant," is a puzzle. Science is our only salvation, and it was a matter of congratulation that I returned in time to apply it to the flower garden, if I was somewhat late for the coarser vegetables.

CHAPTER XIII.

SCIENCE.

I HAD a high appreciation of the superiority of learning in cultivating the earth. Beside the dazzling statements of the brilliant writers on agriculture, the humdrum notions of the plodding workers were little less than disgusting. What is the few bushels of potatoes which an acre yields under common management when compared with the hundreds of barrels which it should give by scientific appliances? Under such manipulation the compost heap becomes a mountain of wealth, and morass a mine of gold. Of course, I discussed these points with Weeville, and impressed upon him frequently the great value of science. Inspired by this feeling, it is not surprising that none of my failures had in the least disheartened me. I was still a firm believer in high art, and studied out every new suggestion that could be made applicable to the restricted area of five acres. I had read all the latest books on the farm, the garden, trees, vegetables, plants, berries, fruits, and every thing whatever which the earth produced for the service of man, except what pertained to the mineral kingdom. No sooner would a seed-store issue a new catalogue than I had it, and devoured the contents for the purpose of discovering novelties; I corresponded with distant florists for whatever they produced as a specialty, or to obtain their descriptive catalogue, and I really began to feel as though I were a man of science myself.

My particular attention had been given to the flowers. This department had been under my charge from the commencement, Patrick confining his exertions to the supply of edibles. I had run through the general list of flowers, had purchased all the hardy bedding sorts which could be obtained ready to be set out, and had at last succeeded in compelling them to grow in spite of their vigorous opposition. I had conquered asters, columbine, anagallis, Jacobœa, snap-dragon, phlox, foxglove, Canterbury bells, hyacinths, tulips, crocuses, balsams, Callirrhoe, coreopsis, pansies, poppies, lobelias, sweet peas, garden rockets, larkspurs, verbenas, zinnias, and many more of the common varieties, besides innumerable shrubs; but, not content with these, my attention was turned to another world, a higher one to overcome, and deeper science to be applied.

This awakening came through a very full and complete catalogue and list of seeds and plants published by a firm strongly indorsed by the ablest periodical on farming in the country, and which I believe in next to the prayer-book. Of course, this approval was sufficient to entitle to implicit confidence what the seedsmen might say, and I fairly devoured the glowing descriptions of new plants that this work—for it contained some one hundred and fifty pages—presented. I made quite a large selection of seeds, and among them ordered a double quantity of a strange plant described in the following enthusiastic manner:

DATURA (TRUMPET-FLOWER), Nat. Ord. *Solanaceæ*.—An ornamental class of plants, many of which possess attractions of the highest order, and are not nearly so extensively cultivated as they ought to be. In large clumps or borders of shrubbery they produce an excellent effect. The roots may be preserved in sand through the winter in a dry cellar. *Half-hardy perennials.*

DATURA WRIGHTII (*Meteloides*).—A splendid variety, with bell-shaped flowers eight inches long, white bordered with lilac, and sweet scented; continues in bloom from July to November; beautiful beyond description; from Asia.

Here was a magnificent future—a perennial, with flowers eight inches long, "beautiful beyond description." To be sure, I was a little troubled about the name. I could not make up my mind positively whether it was "Datura" or "Meteloides." They were both good names, however, and that, in science, is half the battle. Still, accuracy is a weakness of mine, and it was unpleasant to call these new seeds half the time Datura, and the other half Meteloides. But I felt that, under either appellation, they were invaluable, and I carefully concealed the possession of the new treasure, that I might at last have a satisfactory triumph over Weeville, who, with his practical and most incomprehensibly successful mode of gardening, was quite a thorn in my scientific side. The papers inclosing the purchase contained minute directions for its cultivation, and I followed these most exactly, resolved that there should be no failure this time, if the strictest attention could prevent it. I supervised the preparation of the hot-bed personally; I saw that the material was properly turned over and worked, and the mould carefully prepared; and two distinct sowings were made, so that in case any untoward accident happened to one, the other might succeed.

Anxiously I waited the issue, and my exultation may be imagined when both came up. Datura, even in its earliest stages, exhibited its aristocratic extraction. There is usually some little difficulty in distinguishing a youthful weed from a plant by its mere appearance; but Meteloides was peculiarly elegant and graceful. The first leaves were not two coarse lobes, but long, slender, delicate, and refined spears of a pale green color, supported by a tall, spare stalk. They gathered strength slowly, and, under assiduous care, frequent watering, and careful shading from the sun, became robust, and finally put forth the permanent foliage. There were a good many of them; in fact, they took up a considerable share of my hotbed, and they soon began to grow large and strong, till I could hardly wait for the warm weather to transplant them into the garden. This change was also effected with the utmost precaution, dull or rainy days being selected; and so determined was I to oversee every step myself, that a slight rheumatism remains to remind me of the circumstance.

However, my labors were rewarded, and, once established in the garden, the Daturas began to grow vigorously. If they occupied considerable room in the hot-bed, they demanded still more in the open air, and the assurance of a wonderful abundance was no longer questionable, the only doubt remaining as to whether there would be place for the other inhabitants. Still, it was apparent that flowers "eight inches long, of white bordered with lilac, and sweet scented," could hardly be surpassed, and that it was impossible to have too many of a plant which was "beautiful beyond description," and the roots of which could "be preserved in sand through the winter," and secure a succession of loveliness for years to come. As the foliage expanded and the branches spread, the difference between this plant and the others, its neighbors, became more and more apparent. It was certainly remarkable, and, the ground having been doubly enriched to receive it, it grew amazingly.

Precisely at what point in its existence doubts about Meteloides arose in my mind, I can not say; and, although they were pooh-poohed and discarded at first, they pressed themselves upon me, and forced me to notice a very strange and unpleasant resemblance. These suspicions grew stronger as the Daturas grew larger, and when the latter began to overshadow all the other flowers, the former became painfully oppressive. I began to suspect that my new purchase was not all right, and awaited anxiously the appearance of those flowers "eight inches long." To be sure, it was an immense reassurance to recall the words of the catalogue, and to read over the indorsement of the seedsmen in the well-known agricultural paper, which was most severe on humbugs; and I felt that my doubts were so unworthy that I was careful never to mention them, but awaited patiently the *dénouement.* Unfortunately, at this precise moment of suspense, Weeville called to see me; and although I endeavored to distract his attention—for his way was always so painfully abrupt—and tried to beguile him with the seductions of the mint-bed, one of his first questions was,

"Well, how goes on the garden? Have you discovered any new way of growing beans wrong end up, or inducing potatoes to produce a dozen sprouts to every eye?"

I replied that my garden was getting along very well; and when he insisted upon a personal inspection, that he might get a lesson or two in science, as he expressed it, I did my best to lead him to the vegetable department. But the attempt was vain. He spied my strange flowers at once, and hastened directly toward a Datura with an expression of countenance that was far from reassuring.

"What on earth have you got there?" he burst forth, before he was near the plant, so that I, skillfully pretending to misunderstand him, and assuming that his question applied to a shrub near by, replied,

"Oh, that is a spiræa. A handsome one, is it not? Growing finely; it will soon cover the entire path."

"I don't mean that—"

"By the way," I inquired, interrupting him, "have you any egg-plants to spare? Ours are not as successful as they ought to be."

"Yes, yes; plenty. But I want to know why you have filled your garden—"

"Walk this way, if you please," I again broke in. "There's a remarkably pretty double Jacobœa that I should like to show you."

"In a minute; but tell me first—"

"And our Lima beans, they are really remarkable; and such carrots and turnips, to say nothing of many other excellent vegetables."

I was becoming a little incoherent, and not sticking to the absolute and naked truth, for Weeville was not to be moved. He stopped resolutely before a wonderful specimen of Datura, and said positively,

"Before I go any where else, I want to know what you call that?"

"Oh, that," I replied, with affected indifference, "that is a Datura."

As he broke into unpleasantly convulsive laughter, I added, hastily,

"I mean to say Meteloides." As he still appeared unconvinced and somewhat choked with merriment, I further explained: "Datura Wrightii Meteloides;

a plant which ought to be more extensively cultivated; bears flowers eight inches long, white bordered with lilac, sweet scented, beautiful beyond description."

"Beautiful!" he shouted; "sweet scented! Why, that is a stink-weed. If you don't believe me, just touch it."

It was. I am sorry to confess the fact, but my fears and suspicions were confirmed. I had succeeded in producing about a hundred stink-weeds. There is one disadvantage about science, which consists in the difficulty of understanding it. Datura and Meteloides are so little like stink-weed that the common mind could hardly connect the two together, although the latter have sweet-scented flowers eight inches long. Moreover, I had supposed that stramonium was the learned name, but it would appear that science had altered that. It was a good deal of trouble to get rid of those Daturas. I could not touch them, for by either name they smelt equally, although not absolutely sweet. It was out of the question to pull them up, and almost as difficult to cut them down. During the operation of their removal they gave forth an odor which seemed to me quite a satisfactory reason why they were not more "extensively cultivated," and which rivaled the best efforts of the American civet, an animal vulgarly known by a more plebeian name. When they were finally eradicated the garden looked quite bare, and a fresh application had to be made to the florists for bedding plants to fill up the vacancies. I still believe in science, but seedsmen should be more full in their descriptions or more careful in their selections; certainly stink-weeds are not very desirable flowers, even under the romantic name Datura or Meteloides.

CHAPTER XIV.

A SECOND DIGRESSION—FAIRY TALES FOR LITTLE FOLKS.

MY five acres at Flushing were located on the top of a hill called Monkey Hill; why so called I can not imagine, for there was never a monkey seen there since the earliest recollection of the first inhabitant; nor could it have been from the want of monkeys, as that is so common a deficiency on Long Island. To be sure, there is a settlement of Irish on one declivity near the salt meadow; but even supposing that, by a stretch of the imagination, Irishmen can be converted into monkeys, that is of comparatively modern date, whereas our Dutch ancestry named the hill generations back. Nevertheless, the hill is Monkey Hill, and the settlement is Monkey Town.

I wander through Monkey Town occasionally, admire the originality of its Celtic architecture, puzzling myself over the buildings to find out which are pig-pens and which are houses—for the pig-pens are so like houses, and the houses are so like pig-pens, that it is hard to tell them apart—and enter into conversation with my fellow-citizens of Irish extraction. I am very affable. I pat the girls on their towy heads, and praise the boys for stout young lads, in the vague hope that the parents may not tear down my fences, nor let their children rob my future apple-trees or steal my pumpkins.

During one of my visits I was much attracted by an old crone who wore spectacles. Spectacles are not unbecoming to some people; they lend an air of maturity to youth, and even improve an elderly lady reading her Bible; but worn permanently by a very wrinkled old woman, with a very long nose and very sharp chin, they have a bewitching effect that, in Massachusetts, would insure the culprit's early decease at the stake. I made immediate advances to that spectacled female, whose age might have been any where from a hundred and fifty to three hundred, in the firm conviction that her conversation would be interesting and improving; nor was I mistaken, for the intimacy engendered by a few visits induced her to confide in me the following story relative to a small, round, muddy pond, that has neither outlet or inlet, but which is always full, or nearly so, of water, and which lies across the main road over against my premises. I can not give the old crone's language, nor could she probably give the real language of the parties in action, for it was undoubtedly Dutch; nor can I convey an idea of her halting, though impressive manner; but the story, having come direct through the broomstick fraternity, is doubtless true in every particular, and may be entitled

LIVE-GEESE FEATHERS.

On the sloping bank near that little pond there dwelt, ages ago, an old man and his wife. The situation was pleasant, and would have been handsome —for the trees were more numerous then than now —if the edge of the bank had been covered with its natural sod; but the trampling of geese and ducks had long ago worn away the vegetation to the bare earth. The water was not over clear, and the scum that here and there floated about, innoxious as it might be to the feathered tribes, was not agreeable to the human eye. In fact, the pond would have been unceremoniously termed a duck-pond, although it was mainly appropriated to geese. Yes, the old man and his wife made their daily bread by raising geese. Not only did the old fellow count upon the sale of the goose for food, but several times a year did he pluck the feathers; and on a large sign, in whitish though somewhat weather-worn letters, he had inscribed "LIVE-GEESE FEATHERS."

The truth must be told, as it always should, and old Marrott had for twenty years, four times a year, cruelly plucked their feathers from the living geese. With the most unfeeling barbarity, he put them to awful tortures, tearing from their reeking bodies the natural covering—and all that he and his wife might not starve. How diabolical must have been the wretch! Little did he heed the poor creatures when their cries, plainly as words, begged and implored mercy; little did he pause when, finding remonstrance vain, they made violent struggles to escape, and flapped their wings, and dashed themselves about; little remorse did his merciless heart experience provided the feathers were numerous and of good quality; and if two or three died from the torture and exposure, what did he care, provided he could sell their remains for food. Was it not a wonder that he had been permitted to carry on his inhuman practice so long? But his punishment came at last.

Among his flock was one, aged and venerable, that he had owned from the very beginning, and which had been plucked upward of eighty times. In his earlier days that gander had struggled, and cried, and besought like the others, but in time he had come to passive endurance, although there was a peculiar fire in his eye, that, if Marrott had noticed, would have quickened even his dull sense. He had been a noble-looking bird—the lord of the flock—but age and ill usage had worn him away to a huge gaunt skeleton. His body was in many places bare, the feathers had been plucked so often; his proud step had fallen away to an awkward shuffle, and, but for the gleam of his eye, no one would have dreamed he had once been a king of birds, so sorry was his plight. The plucking season had almost come round again, and already the geese—for long experience had accustomed them to the time—began to tremble in their feathers; already they had serious thoughts of rebellion or flight, and their loud cackling whenever their master appeared very clearly evinced their terror.

One night Mother Marrott had gone to the market with a number of eggs to sell, and had left the old man alone. She was not to be back till next day—for it was a long journey to the city in those times, before railroads were invented, and when the traveler had no horse—and, as her husband sat in the evening by the faint, flickering light of the tallow candle, the most painful apprehensions took possession of what must be called his mind. Strange ghost and goose like sounds passed round and round the old house. Ever and anon from the poultry-yard came curious low noises, as of suppressed conversational cackling, and the wind sighed with a hissing sound, while his shadow fell in all sorts of odd and uncouth shapes upon the wall, as little like himself and much like a goose as could be. In fact, it seemed as though there was the dim outline of a goose trying to conceal itself in his shadow. He was afraid to look at it fairly, but he could see from the corner of his eye that it was something uncommon. There was but one refuge—bed; he hastened to undress, but his clothes had never before made such objection to being taken off. He was afraid to pull his shirt over his head—he was confident it would catch round his throat—so he left it on. Amid his trepidation he resolved to keep the light burning; but, just as he went to snuff it, an audible hiss resounded from the chimney corner, and in an instant he snuffed it out. Then he leaped into bed, and hid his head below the bedclothes, glad of the refuge.

There he lay still, while his heart beat so loud that it seemed to shake the room. The unusual noises increased even above its beating, and still more ominous sounds were heard. The windows rattled, the door creaked, the fire crackled, the wind whistled. Horror on horrors! the door opened! unquestionably it swung open, and the cold night air rushed in. For a moment afterward all was silent, then pat, pat, pat went little feet across the floor. Yes, above the rattling and the creaking could his sharpened senses detect the unearthly tread of those little feet—pat, pat, pat. They seemed now to pause before the fire. Pat, pat, pat, they walk to the window. Then pat, pat, pat, they approached the bed. Old Marrott shivered, but it was not with cold this time; old Marrott shrank down, but it was not to avoid the night air.

He hoped he would escape observation; but no; there was a rustle, and something rested on the bed. The old man's breath came thick and fast. Suddenly the covers were dragged from off him, and as he sprang up to a sitting posture a fearful sight met his eyes. There, upon the foot of the bed, stood the old gander, with one end of the bedclothes in his mouth. There he stood, grim and silent, and now the old man saw but too plainly the revengeful glow of his piercing eye. Around and behind him were feathers—millions of feathers—the same that had been plucked from him during his long life. They had all arrived for that night of vengeance. Some had come from ladies' beds and some from lawyers' desks, some from lovers' hands and some from gluttons' teeth. There they were floating to and fro in the air, and awaiting the orders of their parent, the gander.

The gander looked sternly at the trembling culprit, who clasped his hands and tried to think of a prayer; but his prayers had been forgotten long ago. Then it stretched out its neck till its head was close to his, and it uttered a low hiss. That hiss had the sound of a human voice. But what was the old man's dread and fright when the goose drew back and commenced to speak as follows:

"For this many and many a year," he said, and his voice had plainly a foreign accent, "I have lived within your power. I have endured all the cruelties your malice could inflict. What excuse have you to offer?"

The old man's teeth chattered so that he could scarcely reply, while a fresh-sharpened pen from a merchant's hand started forward and enforced the question with a deep thrust.

"Oh! oh!" screamed poor Marrott, his wits on the stretch; "I only did it to get my living."

"What! Hard-hearted man! could you not have stripped us after death, instead of torturing us while alive?" and then three quills fell upon him, and came away dyed in his blood.

"Oh, mercy! I could not obtain enough feathers that way," replied Marrott, scarcely conscious of what he was saying.

"Was it avarice, then? Is that your explanation? Do you imagine that an excuse which rather aggravates your crime?" and a dozen feathers enforced the gander's words, amid the cries of the miserable victim.

"Every one does the same!" he shrieked in his agony.

"If every one else is cruel, is that a reason you should be? Ought you not rather to have drawn a better moral from their vicious example?" and again the plumes plunged into his flesh, for he was but little protected against such an attack.

"Oh, murder! murder! The feathers of dead geese are not worth as much as those of live," he cried out, the torture getting the better of his prudence.

This answer was too unfeeling for the gander and his followers to endure. They dashed, one and all, upon the old man, who leaped from the bed and took to flight. They followed, and now, when they plunged into his body, the feathers remained sticking there. They pursued him round the yard, while he fought with his arms, and cried, and begged, much as the geese had flapped, and fluttered, and cackled before. The rest of the flock joined in the hunt, and bit the flesh from his bare legs, and beat him with their wings, till the old man sank in a swoon. Then they spread their wings, and soared far, far out of sight.

Next day, when Dame Marrott returned, what was her astonishment to find the house-door open, and to see her husband's clothes scattered about upon the floor, while he was nowhere to be found. She called, but there was no answer. The place seemed unusually silent, and there was no noise from the fowls. She went to the poultry-yard; no geese were to be seen. She called them, as if to be fed; they did not come. She began to search, and then she found one poor goose stretched upon the ground, bloody and half dead. What did it mean? She took him up and carried him in, to revive him by the fire. Little did she dream that she bore her husband in her arms. She rubbed and caressed him till he came to himself, and then, for the first, did the old man know what had befallen him. He was changed to a gander; he tried to speak—a loud hiss alone issued from his mouth. He tried to gesticulate—he could only flap his wings. He walked hastily up and down; he pulled at the dame's frock, who was now busied with other things, and he thrust his bill in her lap, till she, alarmed at such proceedings, drove him from the house. How miserable was now his lot! how sorely he repented of his past wickedness! He approached other geese of the neighbors, but they either fled from him, or fell upon and beat him. He was compelled to remain solitary and miserable, with no one to whom he could confide his sorrows.

But the worst was to come. His wife, after wondering what had become of her husband, concluded that "he was such an old goose he had got drowned in the creek;" and, as it was plucking-time, and she had nothing else to divert her mind, she determined to pluck the only one of the flock remaining. Oh, what dreadful torments did the poor gander endure, and from the hands of her he loved! How he shrieked! how he struggled! What agonizing efforts he made to speak, but in vain! The old woman, only too well accustomed to her business, held him fast, and tore out feather after feather; and, although she thought more blood than usual flowed from the wounds, she did not worry herself about that. It was now his turn to endure those tortures he had so often inflicted—tortures tenfold increased from the greater tenderness of his flesh. When the task was finished, he lay bleeding, and agonized, and scarce able to move. He waddled slowly down to the pond, and the cool water assuaged his wounds. But what was his dread, and his wife's delight, when he saw his feathers growing again with astounding rapidity! In two weeks they were quite large, and in two more he was in condition to pluck again. What a life was before him, to be doomed every month to excruciating sufferings, and that from one who was mourning for her husband at every pang she gave him.

But the dame grew rich. In her one goose she had an exhaustless treasure. He cost little to keep, and the more she plucked, the more there was for next month. She built a new house, and then, forgetting her husband, ideas of a fresh marriage suggested themselves to her. There was a young man soon found to marry her for her wealth, and what was her old husband's misery to think that his torments purchased her a new bridegroom! But this husband was a worthless fellow, much given to drink, and, in a fit of intoxication, he killed the old goose, from which all their luxuries flowed. Poverty came upon them, and, ere long, the dame had no feathers to sell, and was forced to dispose of her house and her land, pond included, and to take down the sign of

"LIVE-GEESE FEATHERS."

Whether this story is positively and literally true, I can not say of my own knowledge, not having been born till one or more centuries after it is supposed to have happened; but there are many pieces of corroborative evidence that go to maintain its entire accordance with fact. Whether the geese really spoke is to be doubted, and the conversation may have been merely a dream—the effect of a bad supper on a worse conscience—but that they flew away can not be questioned, for the pond is there, and I have visited it often, and never saw a goose near it. It is well known that feathers are plucked from the living geese, and, as the sign is no longer up, it is fair to presume it must have been taken down. So, with the foundation of the pond, which still exists, to start upon, and with the absence of the sign and the admitted probability of the geese, we have a strong case without the positive assertion of my informant, who insisted she had been there, and whom I shrewdly suspected to be Dame Marrott herself, converted by glamourie from a Dutch vrow into an Irish crone. As this legend lends a double charm and greatly-enhanced value to the property in the neighborhood of the pond, the interests of my five acres and their owner could not permit it to be lost.

CHAPTER XV.

NUISANCES, INHUMAN AND HUMAN.—PETS—THE CHARM OF COUNTRY LIFE.

"MUSQUITOES! You'll never be troubled with them. You may be surprised to hear it, but musquitoes at Flushing never come into the house. They will often be plenty outside, but they disappear the moment your foot touches the piazza. Another strange thing about them is, that they may be abundant in the grass, and, as you walk through, may rise up in thousands, but they seem to be frightened at man, and fly away at once without waiting to bite. It is my opinion they get some other kind of food, and are too well supplied to overcome the instinctive animal repugnance to a human being."

Thus remarked Weeville, in his usual enthusiastic way over every thing that "lives, moves, or has its being" in or about Flushing, and no one who heard him could doubt for a moment his firm conviction in the entire accuracy of his statements. Historic truth, however, compels me to admit that his views were not entirely borne out by experience; for, although Flushing musquitoes have amiable tempers for musquitoes, they do occasionally bite.

But if the musquitoes are not bad in this delectable spot, another torment exists, which, in spite of learned arguments proving its utility to man, is certainly trying—flies are occasionally abundant. Now it may be that flies are great scavengers, and save us from epidemics, and noxious smells, and dangerous vapors, and that their presence is a sure indication of a healthy locality; but in the early morning, when one is in bed, enjoying that most enjoyable season for sleep—the forbidden hours between sunrise and eight o'clock—two or three hundred flies buzzing about, alighting on one's face, crawling into one's nostrils, tickling every inch of exposed skin, are aggravating enough. In saying two or three hundred, I do not wish to be understood as positively confining myself to that number for the reputation of the place and the salability of my five acres of lots. I wish to avoid exaggerating, and there may have been two or three thousand.

After they had routed me out of bed at an hour when there was nothing whatever to do—for the daily papers can not be obtained in Flushing before

NUISANCES, INHUMAN AND HUMAN. 205

half past seven o'clock — they pursued me all day long. They crawled into the cream, they scalded themselves to death in my coffee, they clambered over the butter, dragging their greasy legs heavily and slowly; they planted themselves on my paper if I tried to write; they filled up my inkstand and clogged the ink; they scratched in my hair, selecting the tenderest and least thickly covered spots, and always re-

turning to them after being frightened away; and when, exhausted with loss of rest and worn out with their attacks, I endeavored to take a nap, they fell upon me and banished sleep from my eyes.

"Flies!" said Weeville, when he heard of my miseries; "why do you not kill them off? I used to be troubled with them, but I bought some of the gray fly-paper — Berensohn's lightning-killer — and soon brought matters to an issue. The very first day we killed forty or fifty, and the girl swept them up in the kitchen by tea-cups full: the supply was not equal to the demand, and I have not been waked by a fly since. What a comfort it is to sleep through the morning in peace, and not a single buzz!"

Before night I had the famous death-dealer, and, according to directions, set it out in saucers, covered with a little water, and watched complacently, and with somewhat of an about-to-be-gratified revengeful feeling in my breast, for the result. I waited and waited; the flies buzzed, and crawled, and tickled, but not one went near the fatal saucer; in every part of the room were they except in that spot. They crawled up and down the walls, they perched on the ceiling, they committed suicide in the water-pitcher, they collected in masses on the crumbs lying about, and chased one another around in playful and amatory mood, but touch that saucer they did not. I moved it from place to place, and set it near where they were thickest, but they only flew hurriedly away with louder buzz, as much as to say, "Get out with your old fly-killer." In a rage, I caught some and threw them into the poisoned chalice, but they whisked out again with a shake of their wings, and went off as diabolically busy and buzzy as ever. I poured out some of the water, fearing the attraction was too much diluted; then, finding that that did not answer, I added an extra quantity, but the result was the same. The only part of the room entirely free from flies was the neighborhood of the fly-paper. I was in despair till a happy thought struck me: taking two of the sheets, which are conveniently stuck together at the edges, I laid them over my face and composed myself to sleep. The effect was magical. Not a fly came near me, and my nap was deliciously unbroken.

Next day, Weeville, on hearing my account, abused me because I had not put some sugar in the water; but, as sugar was not mentioned in the direction, it is hardly to be expected a person would divine its necessity. With that addition, the paper afterward killed flies enough; but, unfortunately, the sugar attracted ten where the poison killed one, and recourse was finally had to nets, which kept the breeze and the flies out together,

I have said that Patrick, among his other acquisitions for our second year's operations, had obtained two pups and two kittens. This was with a view to the extermination of the rats and mice that ate our oats and danced nocturnal jigs in the partitions and ceilings of the house. As Patrick explained it, he wanted the dogs to catch the rats, and the cats to catch the mice, which was certainly a fair division of labor; but the former evidently considered that they were merely designed to carry into practice one link in the story of the "House that Jack Built," and devoted their time mainly to worrying the latter. Whether the pups would have caught rats or the kittens mice is hard to tell, as they were altogether too busy worrying or being worried to devote much attention to the chase, and many was the battle waged between the belligerents. The entire science of strategy could be learned from studying the conduct of this feline and canine war, and I have always believed that Grant and Lee had both gone to the cats and dogs to acquire their knowledge. Felis, being the weaker, retires behind her intrenchment of boxes or chairs, and takes advantage of the natural defenses of corners and holes, while canis, being driven to the attack, exhausts his ingenuity in endeavoring to turn his opponent's flank, or to inveigle her from her intrenchments. I called my dogs Gran and Sher (it seemed almost sacrilegious to copy the names literally), and the cats Lee and John.

Gran was a bull-dog, although not of quite pure blood, and my conscience troubled me somewhat on that score; but his grip was most tenacious, and no punishment could make him "sing out;" while Sher was a full-blooded Scotch terrier, as ugly as possible, but a sly little fellow, great on unexpected attacks, and dodging in on exposed places. Apart from his permanent battle with the kittens, and a most inveterate dislike to boys and beggars, Gran was the gentlest of dogs. He would beg for his dinner, and would howl out his affection if asked whether he loved his master and simultaneously offered a piece of sugar, of which he was extravagantly fond. His countenance was expressive of the strongest devotion, and his curly tail had a kindly wag for all his acquaintances. But let a dirty boy appear—and Flushing abounds with this nuisance—or let a beggar attempt to enter the front gate, and Gran went into a paroxysm of rage; his hair bristled up, his tail straightened and became twice its natural thickness, and his eyes glared with the wildest fury. If the offending party carried a bag, his fate was sealed, and many was the time that I had to rush out and interpose to save some tramp from the fate of the gentleman mentioned in Scripture, whose flesh was eaten by dogs. On these occasions Sher was true to himself; and while Gran rushed headlong on the enemy, he would suddenly bounce out from under a bush, or slip round through the fence, and make a diversion in the rear. My dogs were soon a terror to the neighborhood, and a much more effectual protection than patting the children on their heads. To be sure, there were a few drawbacks to set off these advantages. It was difficult to keep any work-people round the place; and I had to pay for a pair of pantaloons that my painter left principally in Gran's mouth ere he could escape up his ladder when a sudden attack caught him unprepared.

There was but one matter in which the kittens and pups all four agreed, and that was to steal whatever they had the slightest fancy for. Milk was the weakness of the kittens, and, provided they could discover any unguarded pan, a truce was declared, and friend and foe united in foraging upon their master. On such occasions they were content to drink together from the same dish in the most amicable way, although the moment the feast was exhausted the cats fled to their intrenchments, without so much as cleaning their whiskers, and hostilities were renewed. The pups preferred meat, and great was the genius exhibited by Sher in obtaining it surreptitiously. He would pretend he was asleep, waiting till the cook's back was turned; or he would ostentatiously go out of the door, and then, slipping back, hide and watch his opportunity. When he obtained it he always divided with Gran, and a bone would occasionally alternate half a dozen times between them ere it was exhausted.

Their playful moods were their most destructive; digging holes was one of their chief pastimes. Why they dug holes I never could imagine; they neither buried nor discovered any hidden treasure; but they worked away with a zeal and patience that would have been most praiseworthy if properly applied. Some of my favorite "herbaceous" plants, as Bridgeman calls them, were rooted up, and my grass-plot—one which I had laid out in a beautiful oval beneath our solitary cedar, and had planted with the most delicate lawn-grass—was fairly honeycombed with burrows. At first I filled these holes and restored my plants, but the pups only seemed to regard this as a challenge to their industry, and immediately proceeded to dig them up again; so I was compelled to let them have their way, although it gave rather a strange appearance to the place, and left an impression that a family of prairie-dogs resided there.

The pups were particularly fond of roaming round the flower garden. When the seeds had pushed their delicate sprouts above ground, I used to walk through the neatly-boxed paths, and admire the thriving way in which every thing was growing. The pups invariably watched for such occasions, and rushed toward me in an apparent burst of affection, bounding up and down over the beds, and dancing with delight on my frailest seedlings. If I took no notice of them, they seized one another by the ears, and, thus coupled, rushed about, sweeping away the flowers in their course; if I scolded them, Sher slipped into the nearest bush, and, lying down in the centre, watched my actions with a wary eye, while Gran, on the other hand, came directly to me, and, seating himself on a bed, looked me honestly and affectionately in the face, while his wagging tail swept away the sprouting plants by dozens.

Sher was particularly fond of a gilia; its delicate leaves seemed to please him both as a bed and a hiding-place, and he soon rolled the life out of it; if I charged upon him, he fled, taking refuge in some other bushy plant; and when I did catch him, he would not walk, but insisted upon being dragged in a most destructive manner from off the bed. If I took hold of Gran he retained his sitting posture, which was almost equally injurious. I soon found my only plan was to match my cunning against theirs, and, the moment they appeared, to rush out of the garden, calling them "good dogs," which was a falsehood of the blackest dye, and pretending I was ready for a romp. By this means they would be induced to follow me with great hilarity, and occasionally forget to go back; but I lost much of my enjoyment of the garden.

When not busy with the flowers, they devoted themselves to the vegetables; Gran was delighted with hunting "hop-toads," as children call them, and as these abounded in our five acres, and were particularly fond of hiding in the water-melon patch, he hunted it over and over again, fairly plowing it up with his nose, crushing the vines, tearing the leaves to pieces, and breaking off the fruit. If he had killed the toads his proceedings might have come to an end with the exhaustion of the game; but he was too tender-hearted for this, and only pushed them with his nose to make them jump. He pursued this exciting sport till the water-melons were almost ruined, while Sher devoted himself mainly to hiding under the okras or among the carrots, and darting out at any passers-by in a playful mood. In the course of his strategic movements he broke down most of the brittle okras, and trampled rows of string-beans into the earth.

They had seen Patrick chase the chickens from the garden, and, having constituted themselves his adjutants, proceeded to keep the sacred precincts clear of these unholy intruders. Never would a wandering pullet or youthful rooster step within the fatal bounds but the two dogs would dart out with loud yelps, and would frequently follow her or him, naturally bewildered, and not knowing which way to escape, several times round the garden, over the beds and through the vegetables, doing more harm in five minutes than an entire brood of chickens would do in a month. It was in vain that we endeavored to explain to them that zeal was dangerous; and their manner of self-congratulation, and of demanding approval when they had finally succeeded in ejecting the trespasser, disarmed blame or correction.

There was one idiosyncrasy in Patrick's mind—he never could punish an animal. If the pups destroyed an entire bed, or broke down a dozen plants, he would only utter an exclamation or two of horror and reproach, and then add, apologetically, "Ah! the poor bastes do not know any better." This threw the duty of correction upon my shoulders, and I never was a subscriber to that horrible doctrine that punishment must not be inflicted in anger. There is something fiendish in a person nursing up his wrath, and then, with deliberate cruelty, venting it upon child or pet who has been trembling for hours with dread anticipation. When the pups had dug up some favorite and expensive plant, or crushed my only plantation of some pet seed, and when I was naturally in a towering rage, I could fall upon them and drive them howling to some secret place of safety; but when, after an hour's delay had dissipated my passion, Gran would approach with deprecating wag and loving smile, and Sher, following more cautiously, would lick his hairy chops in a contrite way, it went against my very nature to beat them. Therefore, although the pups met with some cuffs, and occasionally received the blow of a well-directed stone, they were not punished with absolute regularity, had it a good deal their own way with the place and its surroundings, and inflicted no little damage upon the growing crops.

CHAPTER XVI.

BUTTER-MAKING.—SEEDS AND THE DEVIL.

THERE is one advantage about the country that gives it a great superiority over the town. In it you have every thing so fresh—fresh vegetables, fresh milk, fresh eggs, fresh poultry, and fresh butter. You always feel sure that nothing is old or stale. We had not yet tried making butter, but the other articles we had enjoyed in their pristine excellence, although some ignorant visitors from the city pretended that all of those which were sold in the Flushing stores were brought from the New York markets. I had been accustomed to buying butter in the village, but the Flushing farmers do not seem to have the knack of making fresh butter. My purchases had not been altogether satisfactory, and occasionally I obtained a rancid conglomeration of fatty matter that was far from inviting. When more than ordinarily disgusted, I had brought a supply home from Fulton Market, where it was to be had both better and cheaper; but as my friends, who met me in the cars, invariably inquired what I had in my tin kettle, and wanted to know whether I had gone out for a day's work and taken my dinner-pail along, I grew ashamed, and determined thereafter to make my own butter.

To say that I was utterly unacquainted with butter-making was simply to admit that I had been born and reared in the city; and, except for some early reminiscences of an enthusiastic youth passing his summer amid rural pleasures, and helping the tired and rosy-cheeked dairy-maid, I knew nothing whatever on the subject, and did not even know in what scientific work to look for the needful instruction, as nothing satisfactory was to be found in "Bridgeman" or "Ten Acres Enough." A churn was to be used, that was clear; but whether the milk was churned or the cream, or how long it required, or what other mysteries were involved, I could not tell.

The first necessity, therefore, was to have a churn, and to obtain this I stopped in at one of the numerous stores in and near Fulton Street, where agricultural implements are sold. I inquired falteringly if they had churns for sale, not being certain that these came under that designation, and a good deal confused at the mass of curious implements and wonderful pieces of mechanism which were scattered about.

K

"Certainly," said the polite clerk; "we might say that we have the only churn, properly so called, for it alone does the work as it should be done. You probably know," he continued, as he led the way up stairs toward the fourth story, "the scientific principles which govern the rapid production of butter. The oxygen of the air is brought in immediate contact with the oleaginous particles of the milk, the lactic acid is developed, the curd and whey are separated, and the butter is crystallized, so to speak. Here," he said at last, when we had reached the highest floor, and, after conducting me between a hundred strange and complex machines, stopped before one that more nearly resembled a modern ice-cream freezer than any thing else, with the addition of a crank and a few extra cog-wheels, "here is the Patent Duplex Elliptic Milk Converter, the only true and perfect churn. You pour the milk in"—[ah! thought I to myself, it is the milk that is churned, after all]—"you turn this handle; by a simple arrangement of multiplying cogs, the dasher is revolved at great speed, the air is distributed through every part of the mass, and brought in contact with every molecule composing it. The lactic acid is generated—but I need not explain further to one who evidently understands the subject so thoroughly as yourself."

"Is there no danger of the machine's getting out of order?" I inquired mildly, not, however, disclaiming the compliment, and much impressed by this display of thorough scientific attainment on the part of my informant.

"None whatever. Observe the dasher."

With that he jerked off the cover and lifted out the part referred to.

"It is armed with flanges, which revolve between the projecting knives, or plates, fastened to the sides of the tub. They thoroughly agitate the milk, which is thrown from one to the other, and never allowed to rest. The effects are truly wonderful. The exertion is the minimum; the results are the maximum. No more sour cream; no more rancid butter. A child can produce a pound of butter from a quart of milk in the short space of a minute and a half."

By this time, between the revolving of the wheels and the man's incomprehensible conversation, I was in a dazed state, and may not remember accurately his statements. I was only clear on one point, and that was that the Duplex Elliptic Milk Converter, although evidently the perfection of science, was too grand for my wants.

"Have you nothing simpler?" I inquired, faintly.

"Nothing can be simpler," was the decided response; "here you have a crank; there, a few iron wheels; inside, the dasher. The price is moderate; one that would do the work of a dairy would be only fifty dollars. That amount could be saved in a summer."

"I should like to inquire farther," I hastily answered; and, hurrying down stairs, in spite of remarks about acids and oxygen, nitrogen, caseine, and a dozen other scientific compounds, I escaped from the store. There is always a dreadful feeling of shame connected with not purchasing when one enters a store and asks for an article. It seems as though you were getting credit and making a display on false pretenses. The manner of the attendant suggests a doubt of your honesty, and any little compliments he may have paid you are manifestly taken back at once, and contempt usurps the place of esteem.

After pausing to recover my breath and my courage, I entered the nearest place of a similar character and made the same inquiry.

"Yes, sir; we have a churn of a most approved and successful description. There," he continued, as the clerk brought me face to face with a still stranger-looking machine, more like the walking-beam of a steam-engine than my early recollections of a churn, "there you have simplicity itself. In it you go back to first principles. You wind up a spring—"

"A spring!" I exclaimed.

"Undoubtedly. No one thinks of using manual power in these times. The dashers are secured to each end of this bar, and as one rises while the other falls, there is no loss from the attraction of gravitation. We call this the Hippo-opticon."

"The Hippo-opticon, did you say?" I inquired, wonderingly.

"Yes; the name is derived from two Greek words, *hippo*, a horse, and *opticon*, sight; because it has the strength of a horse and the eye of intelligence. It works without care or superintendence. When once started it runs of itself. The cream—"

"The cream!" I muttered to myself, having supposed that I had just discovered that milk was churned.

"The cream is placed in these two receptacles; the dashers fall regularly and slowly."

"Slowly!" I exclaimed, still more surprised, remembering the praises I had heard of excessive speed.

"Churning must be done slowly; that is the best established law. There must be deliberation and regularity."

"What is your opinion," I inquired, "of the Patent Duplex Elliptic Milk Converter?"

"Then you have seen that worthless contrivance! It could not have deceived an experienced farmer like yourself. Why, that whirligig is the most utterly useless affair conceivable. It is forever out of order; the flanges bend, the cogs break. Whatever you do, don't buy that. In ours you have primitive simplicity and perfect security."

At this point a brilliant idea entered my mind, and, taking my departure without even waiting to ask the price of this wonderful invention, I hurried back to the first store. Thrusting my head in at the door, and not daring to advance farther lest I should be overwhelmed by a second avalanche of learned terms, I inquired of the smiling clerk, who evidently saw the certainty of a customer in my return, what he thought of the Hippo-opticon.

"The Hippo-opticon!" he laughed; "that old fogy concern that winds up with a spring? My opinion simply is that it will never make butter at all. It never has yet, and it never will. They could not humbug a gentleman of your discernment with that attempt to return to the antiquated days of our forefathers. The Patent Duplex—"

"Thank you!" I shouted, as I slammed to the

door, and fled without waiting to hear farther. The selection of a churn was evidently an intricate matter. It was a practical affair, in which intellectual research would not help me, and recourse must be had to Weeville. As soon as I returned to the country I sent for him, and inquired which was the proper churn to use, and what was the proper thing to put in it.

"Well," he said, deliberately, "the art of making butter is yet in its infancy; the principles that control it are not fully understood. Great cleanliness is a prime requisite; the dairy must be well ventilated; electricity is very injurious. In Switzerland they do not allow women to take part in any of the operations, even in milking the cows, on account of their possessing more electricity than men."

"Oh!" I broke forth in despair, "I give it up; it is altogether too complicated a matter—"

"Nonsense," said Weeville, suddenly recovering himself; "the old-fashioned ordinary churn is the best; I will send you one. You must use cream, and there is no difficulty so long as proper regard is paid to cleanliness."

With that he left me. His suggestions about electricity were alarming. I had often felt the electrical power of the female sex. I had received many dangerous shocks from them; the touch even of their hands had often produced palpitations and electrical phenomena of the strangest kind. There could be no anticipating what might be the result if the cream was affected by their presence. While I was hesitating what to do, I suddenly thought of Patrick. There was nothing electrical about him. He might be dirty—his hands and face usually were—but there was no other danger. He was called at once, and told to milk the cow himself in future, and be sure to wash his hands and face first; to which directions he gave a surprised assent, wondering, no doubt, at the sudden interest his master evinced in his personal appearance. I took charge of the dairy myself, to exclude all possibility of electrical phenomena, and skimmed the cream carefully. Cushy had been falling off lately for some incomprehensible reason, having done so well for eighteen months; and when, at the end of a week, the churn arrived, it seemed ludicrously large for the small bowlful of cream that had been collected — not much more than a pint in all. Patrick, when I called upon him to wash his hands and set to work, burst forth with the astonished inquiry,

"Sure yer honor does not want me to churn that little speck ov crame in this big tub. It would get lost intirely."

BUTTER-MAKING.

"But, Patrick," I replied, "this cream must be churned at once." This conclusion was not any deduction of science, although it was announced in an authoritative tone, intended to impress Patrick with my vast experience and thorough knowledge of the subject. To state how I arrived at my opinion, it is sufficient to say that my nose assured me of it. The weather was warm, and the dairy was merely a closet in the cellar, springs and brooks not being numerous in my territory.

"Well, then, yer honor, let me make a nate little churn out ov a ginger-pot there is in the cellar, with the lid ov a salt-box for dasher, and the piece ov a broom for handle. That will be the doin' ov it."

"Just as you please, Patrick," I answered, entirely convinced of the inadequacy of the cream to the occasion; "only be sure and make me a good article."

"Indade and I will do that same, and I'm sure yer honor will be mightily plased. Let me aloon for that."

Shortly after, Patrick produced a queer-looking extemporized churn that, although odd enough in appearance, was manifestly better adapted to the emergency than the enormous affair that Weeville had sent me, apparently supposing that I was about to set up a public dairy. I expected a friend to dinner that day, and gave especial directions that the results of the churning were to come on the table as a surprise to my guest.

When the dinner was served, I was delighted with the whiteness of the fresh butter, that spoke so well for its purity. Without saying a word, I helped my friend liberally, and then awaited the result. How I enjoyed, by anticipation, his enjoyment of so rare a delicacy! I could scarcely wait for him to taste it before explaining how it was obtained. He looked at it curiously, then spread some on his bread and tried it, then ate the bread without. Hastily taking a piece and tasting it, I no longer wondered at his conduct, but, turning to the maid, sternly demanded how she dare put such stuff on the table.

"Oh, never mind," said my friend; "these things will happen in the country, where you do not have any markets to go to. I often taste bad butter when I am out of town, although not often so bad as this; but I can do without very well."

When dinner was over, I visited my man, and inquired of him, rather reproachfully than angrily,

"Patrick, what was that you made? Was it cheese, or was it butter? It was very bad as either; but which was it?"

"Sure, yer honor," he replied, scratching his head, "I don't rightly know meself; but the crame was spoilt intirely, and I did the best I could."

"Patrick," I answered, "I am afraid you are electrical, after all."

This attempt was but a sort of interlude, and I kept my mind mainly on the various productions of the earth.

"Weeville," I said one day, in early fall, when the first cold snap had thrown a tinge of brown over much of my garden, "how do you manage to collect the flower-seeds for use next spring?"

"Why, my dear boy," he replied, gayly, "that is easy enough: dry them a little, put them in bags labeled, and set them aside in a dry place, where the mice can not get at them to make a daily meal at your expense."

"I do not refer to that part; the books on gardening speak of that, but they give no directions for gathering the seed. I have studied Bridgeman, Rand, and the rest of them, but they nowhere tell you when or how to collect the seed."

"My dear fellow, you surely would not expect Bridgeman to tell you how to save seeds; that is his occupation, and a pretty fool he would be to let out all the secrets of his trade."

"Then he had no business to write on gardening," I added, earnestly; for I have an immense idea of duty, and a high standard for the obligations of authorship; "a man who publishes a book, and retains any knowledge on the subject of which he treats for his own purposes, is a scoundrel and a cheat; he is false—"

"Now, now," interrupted Weeville, soothingly, "don't get on your high horse; remember human nature. A pretty notion it would have been if Bridgeman had enabled all his customers to do without him, and perhaps set up in the seed-business themselves."

"I can only say, then, that he had no right to take upon himself the honors of authorship; there is no justification for his assuming the place of instructor when he was merely a self-seeker. His book, then, is simply an advertisement."

"Call it what you please, but do not get excited. Borrow his catalogues, which contain much useful information, and for which he charges nothing, but do not abuse a hard-working man, striving to get ahead in the world."

"Very well, then. To come back to my difficulties—I want to know when I am to gather the seeds; they only ripen in small quantities, and, if left, are scattered and lost."

"Oh, you must watch your chance; stick to it; 'here a little, and there a little;' do not be impatient."

"The pods of phlox burst the moment they turn yellow, and, ere I notice them among the mass of those still green, they have spilled their contents; the gilia are so small that I can not find them at all; the mignonnette really does not seem to bear seed; and the capsules of the portulaca have to be picked one at a time, and are so low that it almost breaks my back to bend down to them. How is it that you manage?"

"I never have any trouble; I go through my garden daily."

"To come to a point—what do you do about the phlox?"

"You must be on the alert, and save all you can."

"Now, Weeville," I said, sternly, for he was in the act of buttoning up his coat to go, as though the discussion were over, "I do not believe you know any thing about it."

"What—what—what's that you say?"

"I do not believe you are any better acquainted with the right mode of gathering seeds than I am."

"Well," he replied, as he went out of the door, with a pleasant smile, "the fact is, I do generally get a new supply every year from Thorburn."

Before I had fully recovered from my surprise at this discovery, and when I was remembering how, every year, the oldest farmers and gardeners were to be seen running into the seed-stores to buy what they should have saved if they had known how, Patrick thrust his head in at the door.

"Can I spake to yer honor a moment?"

"Certainly, Patrick."

"And is it thrue, what Mr. Weeville says, that the devil's been seen on the earth?"

"It is so alleged in the papers," I replied, "and you know whatever is stated there must be true."

"Yes, yer honor," he answered, evidently referring in his own mind to a temporary connection of mine with that palladium of freedom. "And sure," he continued, as he approached cautiously, "and what is he like?"

"He is described as being forty feet high, spitting fire from his mouth and nostrils, and with huge horns over his eyes."

"That's awful intirely; but there's prophecies in the Good Book that he should be let loose on the earth, but I didn't think it was to be quite yet. Was it far from here that he was?"

"Yes, more than a thousand miles."

"Sure and that's pleasant, for it ain't likely he'll get this far."

"That is not so certain," I replied, to lead him on. "He has a habit of going up and down on the earth."

"But it would take him a long time to travel that distance."

"The devil, if it really was he, could go a thousand miles in an instant."

"Could he, now? Well, I suppose he don't go by rail, more especially like the one that runs from

New York to Flushing. Perhaps he travels on the telegraph wires, that, they say, takes a letter along so fast you can't see it. Well, well, if he comes this way, all I have to say is, he'll get great gatherins in Flushing."

CHAPTER XVII.

SUCCESS OF THE YEAR.

THE agricultural books all tell us that, at the close of the season, we should look back and review the work that we have accomplished, comparing it with previous results, or studying where improvements could be effected. Our second year was certainly a great advance upon the first, as the former might be said to have been rather a case for what the merchants call profit and loss—all loss and no profit, so far as actual production is concerned. The previous attempt had resulted in raising absolutely nothing, whereas our subsequent one had raised a great deal; we had much to show for it, although not always exactly what we wanted. There was ample room for improvement, and there were abundant errors manifestly requiring correction. We did not need an acre of onions, that was perfectly clear, as the servants could consume but a limited quantity, which fell off rapidly when they were told they could have all they wanted, and the residue did not seem to have a positive market value, Patrick vainly offering them at any price to every market-man in Flushing; so it was evident that we should not require as many the ensuing season.

Onions are rather a pretty vegetable, and grateful for the least care. They grow readily; in fact, like the would-be "butcher boy," they are bound to do it. They come up so well that they come clear up above ground in their effort, and show their luscious yellow or white bulbs above the surface. When these first began to swell I proceeded to earth them over, fearing lest their nakedness should expose them to injury; but, as the plot devoted to their service was rather large, and Patrick utterly refused to assist me, being invariably too busy whenever I called upon him to help cover the onions, and insisting that "they didn't nade it at all, at all, and that it was ruinin' them I was intirely," I finally abandoned the attempt. It was some time ere my fears for the result were removed, and the discovery made that onions could take care of themselves. It is a pity egg-plants do not grow as obstinately as onions; they do not, however, nor do most other good things.

Peas are a profitable crop—that is, if they are not dwarfs, or do not go to leaf, as ours did; and there are many different kinds—so many that the novice in gardening is somewhat puzzled to choose. Fortunately, by Weeville's advice, we had made an excellent selection, and by changing the acre of onions into an acre of Daniel O'Rourkes we might possibly have enough for the family. As I have mentioned before, the O'Rourkes are not profuse bearers; it may be called a rather lucky chance if they bear any thing but leaf, and consequently it is not in a monetary sense that they are profitable; the benefit they confer is in enabling one to crow over one's city visitors. The dwarfs are not desirable. They constituted our principal stock, and, useful as they might be in the penance line, as edibles they compare unfavorably with pebbles.

We had an immense quantity of beets, and had experimented in divers ways of cooking them. We had them boiled, baked, stuffed, and roasted, hot, cold, pickled in vinegar, and even fried, but through it all they were "dead beets." I had serious ideas of trying to extract sugar from them; but when Patrick informed me that Dandy Jim approved of their flavor, I gave them over to his care. Our pole-beans, which are good for pork and beans—if any Christian eats that dish and lives—were also extremely successful. The Limas bore a few pods, but that was after we returned to the city; Patrick, however, said they were excellent. Our spinach was so abundant that I should have turned Cushy into it if I could have restricted her attentions to that alone. The cucumbers were very numerous, our cabbages innumerable, and our cauliflowers nowhere.

It was clear that this must be changed. The Limas must be made to emulate the pole-beans, the spinach, beets, and onions must be kept down to proper limits, the cucumbers and cabbages must be eliminated, and the cauliflowers encouraged. How to effect these changes, however, was not entirely clear to my mind.

Our corn grew remarkably well. Fresh sweet corn is a dish of which I am particularly fond; it is luscious, healthful, and appetizing; it contains much milk—the human being's natural nourishment; it is excellent boiled or roasted on the cob, stewed in milk, or mixed with beans into succotash; even corn juice is good occasionally—but that requires age. Patrick had planted a goodly lot of it. I watched the stalks rise and the broad leaves spread out with infinite pleasure. The ears formed with their long silky tops, and swelled, as they reached maturity, like a budding maiden. It was with great anticipations that we awaited our first meal of new corn. This was admirably cooked, and came on the table smoking hot, each cob enveloped in its steaming green cuticle, but somehow the taste did not prove so agreeable as we had expected. Thinking that it might be too young, I told Patrick not to pick any more for a day or two. The next trial was even more unsatisfactory —it had absolutely no flavor whatever. Feeling there must be something wrong, with sinking heart I cross-questioned Patrick, and discovered that he did not know there was any difference between sweet corn and the common kind, and had planted a quantity of that which he was using for the horses. I never ascertained what became of it, but we did not try it again on the table.

Our asparagus was gone without redemption. The few spears that struggled up into existence reached a partial state of forwardness; but association with Patrick's planting of turnips appeared to disgust them, and they lay down and died with hardly an effort. Our trees succeeded excellently; they were unusually large, and had cost an extra price, as the nurseryman, when I bought them, assured me that they would bear fruit the first year. They stood the blasts of winter bravely. In spring they put out their leaves, and even burst into occasional flower, but they did not go so far as bearing fruit. They appeared to have some misunderstanding of the principal object of their existence, and did not come up to the promise made for them on their purchase, and by them afterward. As shade-trees they did not amount to much, and even as ornaments they were rather thin; but as fruit-bearers they were a total failure.

Our strawberries had rather surpassed expectation. The first lot, it is true, had died out, but those planted in the spring seemed to feel called upon to redeem the good name of the race. They grew admirably, and not only covered themselves with blossoms, but actually bore fruit—not very luxuriantly, but much more abundantly than I had any reason to anticipate. We had quite a bowlful of them—the red, firm, ripe berries being a delicious contrast to the soft, faded, stale things that are sold to us in the city. When these were picked, the vines were still covered with green fruit, and I expected to have many a dessert from them. I am a great admirer of strawberries—and so are chickens—in spite of the crisp little seeds that somewhat injure them. They have just the proper amount of acidity to render them piquant when compounded with sufficient sugar. Raspberries are too sweet, and blackberries have not sufficient delicacy of flavor, so that I prefer strawberries. But, unfortunately, as I remarked above, so do chickens.

After our first taste I visited the garden hopefully every morning, but was much surprised to find none of the green berries become ripe. They disappeared gradually, and I was greatly at a loss to understand the reason. I knew that Gran was fond of strawberries, but he was an honest dog. You might trust him with untold strawberries, and he would not touch one without permission. He might howl for them until he would drive his master crazy, but, although his howlings were ineffectual, he would not steal. Sher was less trustworthy, but he did not like the acid berries. The pigs could not get out, nor Cushy get in; so that the diminution was a mystery to me, until, happening to rise one morning quite early, I discovered our entire flock of chickens busy in the strawberry-patch, and, driving them out, I noticed the remains of several fine ripe berries. This explained the difficulty. There was no place where we could cage the chickens; in fact, as the berries were mostly consumed, to do so would be rather late, and I had nothing for it but to see my favorite fruit "grow small by degrees and beautifully less," amid the early "clucks" of delight that thereafter suggestively broke in upon my morning slumbers, until the entire plot was bare.

From this adventure two deductions were to be

drawn: one, that I must plant more of these energetic vines; the other, that I must build a chicken-coop. The latter would cost heavily, probably more than many years' supply of both berries and chickens; and, to save the expense of applying to the nurseries for the former, I must encourage our own vines to run and propagate. To effect this, when July drew toward a close, and they put out suckers in every direction, I pinned these down with small forked sticks, so as to compel them to take root. This was an original idea of my own, of which I was particularly proud. Weeville ridiculed it, saying that there would be young plants enough without that trouble; but I determined to help Nature—which the doctors have lately ascertained is the true principle in encouraging human plants to grow and discouraging them from dying. The work kept me quite busy, for it was astounding how many runners started off and how fast they ran. They took root finely, and soon made the entire patch a mass of flourishing plants. They grew and grew, and interlaced and twined round one another, and, unfortunately, the weeds grew with them, till, when I undertook to transplant them in the fall, I could not tell the old plants from the young. This was rather unlucky; for, unless the old stools, as they are called, were preserved, there would be but a slim crop the following year. Nevertheless, I tried in vain to distinguish the parents from their healthy children, and at last had to direct Patrick to dig out as many as he wanted indiscriminately, and then to cut paths through the residue at regular intervals, regardless of what might be in the way. The next year will show the result, for which I was prepared to wait with due patience.

The second season of my life in the country having closed, and the new year, with relaxation from agricultural pursuits, being upon us, I proceeded to make up my annual exhibit of the result. The investments of my previous year had not turned out well; the asparagus and strawberries failed utterly, and my garden had been a virgin soil when it was attacked in the spring. But this season there was every reason to be satisfied with the result; the productions, although not exactly such as a gourmand would prefer, were abundant; the flowers had been a grand success, some of them far surpassing the wildest anticipations; and the vegetables did no discredit to the soil, although they did not reflect much honor on Patrick's judgment. The fact had been clearly established that there was only needed the eye and mind of the master to produce a highly

L

creditable result. It could not be questioned that a place which would grow such wonderful pumpkins, and such vast expanse of onion, and such early and abundant squashes, would also, if properly managed, be as fertile of egg-plants, cauliflowers, and the other higher classes of vegetables. There was no probability of my again visiting the Old World, and I should be able to devote undivided attention to my horticultural pursuits.

As with the previous year, it is not an easy matter to make out the accounts satisfactorily; there were items that were of questionable relationship toward investment or yearly expenditure; there were kinds of profit difficult of estimation, and, as usual, there were sundry matters altogether forgotten. If there is any one point more important than another in recording the experiences of an individual in any pursuit, when these experiences are to be the guide of others, it is absolute exactness in figures and calculations. I have, therefore, been exceedingly careful, and devoted much consideration to every item ere it was inserted, and I flatter myself that the following statement may be relied upon confidently:

INVESTMENT ACCOUNT.—DEBIT.

Cost of premises	$15,000
Three hundred loads of fertilizer	180
Strawberry plants	3
New teeth	50
Dandy Jim	450
Total	$15,683

INVESTMENT ACCOUNT.—CREDIT.

Value of premises	$16,000
Dandy Jim	50
New teeth	100
Strawberry bed	50
Total	$16,200

YEARLY EXPENSES.—DEBIT.

Asparagus	$ 6 00
Seeds	10 50
Subscription to Skating-pond	10 00
Damage to wagon	50 00
Total	$76 50

YEARLY RECEIPTS.—CREDIT.

One quart of strawberries	$ 50
One hundred bushels (estimated) of onions	50 00
Ten egg-plants	2 50
One peck Daniel O'Rourke peas	2 00
One thousand squashes	100 00
Five hundred cucumbers	20 00
One hundred pumpkins	25 00
Five cauliflowers	2 50
Fifty bushels of tomatoes	25 00
Beets, beans, turnips, etc.	50 00
Total	$277 50

There are some items in the foregoing accounts that require explanation. The manure was included in permanent capital, because it went into the ground, became incorporated with it, and added just so much additional value to it. The strawberries, having now proved successful, ceased to be a current expense, but entered into the total cost. The new teeth referred to are not for the rakes, as might be supposed, but for myself. Having heretofore mentioned some of Dandy Jim's peculiarities, I omitted an explanation of our last association and final separation. I was not fond of driving the gallant steed—so gallant that he usually danced twenty feet to one side, and stood on his hind legs whenever he saw the dress of a woman—but I was occasionally forced to make use of his services. The train happening to give out, and being pressed to attend to some business in town, I had him harnessed, and, with some misgivings, commenced my journey toward the city. By great care and discretion, I managed to make my way through the village, which he cleared at full run, in consequence of a sudden whistle from a locomotive attached to a dirt train; over the bridge, where he shied from one side to the other, grazing both the wheels against the heavy plank balustrade; along Jackson's Avenue, where he bounced up and down on passing every market-wagon or hay-cart; on board the ferry-boat, to which he was only constrained by violent abuse and the physical strength of several of the hands of the boat, and where he amused himself by pawing steadily, and occasionally backing on the horse directly behind, and thus causing much excitement, bad temper, and coarse language during the entire trip; and fairly on the stone pavements of the city streets.

By this time I had lost all fear, having resigned myself to perfect recklessness, like the man who, after being exposed a thousand times to death, no longer dreads it; and I drove up Thirty-fourth Street, across the tunnel at Fourth Avenue, and into Fifth Avenue, as though there was no such thing as peril in my path. Down our fashionable thoroughfare I proceeded, assuming rather a jaunty and professional air; I squared my elbows, held my whip in my hand, taking great care not to touch Dandy Jim, however, and looked round at the foot-passengers, as much as to say, "I am not afraid to drive this wild animal; I do it every day." Unfortunately for the triumph of my assumptions, there was a piece of paper lying directly in our path.

Now Dandy Jim has an objection to paper, why I never could discover; but paper, white or brown, newspaper or blank paper, leaves or letters, is to him a thing of horror—his very soul revolts at it. It certainly never could have done him any injury—it is, except as a vehicle of slander, so perfectly harmless —but he seemed to hold it in abject terror. This idiosyncracy was well known to me, but, unfortunately, my mind was so occupied with the effect I was producing that I did not notice the exciting cause. To aggravate the difficulty, just as we approached the objectionable article, and when my peculiar animal might have consented to pass by with a reasonable amount of self-restraint, a sudden gust blew it directly under his feet. If paper was his detestation, moving paper was a monstrosity magnified fifty fold; he reared up on his hind legs, made one bound sideways full thirty feet, and then, stopping suddenly, slipped on the pavement, and fell flat on his side.

Exactly what happened to me I never could determine. I seemed to be flying; next I beheld a splendid coruscation of fire-works; and then I awoke to find myself stretched at full length in the street, with a bloody nose and a scarcity of front teeth. Dandy Jim regained his feet more quickly than myself, ran away, smashed the wagon, as was his wont, and wound up by getting shut in by stages and carts, when he was ignominiously led away captive by a stalwart policeman. I gathered myself up as well as I could, and went home in a dilapidated state. This led to my selling Dandy Jim and buying a set of false front teeth; the former brought precisely what it cost to pay for the latter.

Thus it was that I overcame a prejudice that had long beset me against the artificial productions of manufacturing dentistry. This objection exists in the minds of many persons, although nothing can be more unfounded. If there is any thing that is an utterly miserable failure, it is the natural set of teeth.

From almost the hour when we come into the world, until the time when we quit it, or so long as a stump or root remains, our teeth are a source of annoyance to us. They have to be cut, and then pulled out, that they may "cut and come again." As babies, we are "never ourselves" for the cutting of our teeth; when we grow older we wish we were any body else, from the misery they cause us. They ache, and decay, and break; they come out when they should stay in, and stay in when they should come out; they torture and torment us till we only get rid of them with life itself.

On the other hand, the artificial teeth never pain the possessor, rarely break, and, if broken, are easily replaced; are readily cleaned, do not fall out, but can be removed at pleasure. They are infinitely handsomer than their ugly, irregular, uneven, discolored, and dirty prototypes. These exquisite productions of art are made of a delicate, pearly shade of white; they form a perfect row of well-proportioned beauty, undistinguishable from the genuine article, their very gums matching and closely fitting the natural flesh beneath them; they never inflict a torturing tooth-ache, driving man crazy with pain, and keeping him sleepless the long, dreary nights; they require no filling—an operation that the unfortunate possessor of living teeth dreads only less than the rack itself; and they do not have to be pulled out, with an agony comparable to the effect of drawing the entire brain out through the hole at the roots.

From my experience before and since my accident, I should certainly advise my fellow-creatures to have as little to do with real teeth as possible, and to substitute the imitation as soon as they can. There may be a certain amount of suffering in having teeth, and especially sound ones, extracted, but the satisfaction of being finally rid of the troublesome things more than pays for the temporary annoyance. A natural set will become dirty in spite of endless scrubbing with the tooth-brush; some are invariably longer than others; there are projections and depressions; wherever they lap, tartar settles; inside it is impossible to get at them at all, and they compel a half-yearly interview with the dentist, from which one comes away greatly unnerved. Their substitutes are a great improvement to one's personal appearance, and never cause the slightest inconvenience, besides saving hours in cleaning, that, in a long life, amount to an aggregate of years. The new teeth were so far superior to those that they replaced, that they are valued on the credit side of the account at a hundred dollars, showing a clear profit of one hundred per cent. In fact, I regard this discovery as one of the most valuable, if not the very most valuable, of the results of my country experience.

The premises are set down at an increase of one thousand dollars, and, if my readers had seen the difference between a bare tract of land and a garden blooming with beauty, odorous with fragrance, and smiling with abundance, they would have felt that the improvement was stated at too low a rate. The strawberries are also put at a large advance upon the prime cost; but a thriving bed of this excellent fruit, bidding fair to supply the wants of the entire household, to gratify friends, and to supply the place of costlier desserts, was well worth a round sum of money. It certainly cost me much care and anxiety; it had failed once, and threatened at first to give out the second time, but finally had proved an absolute success, and was already becoming the parent of other plantations.

Among the items of yearly expense will be found included a charge for entrance-fee to the skating-pond. This may at first seem to be more of a luxury than an actual necessity, but, as it was clear that I should not have incurred it if I had not been in Flushing, I put it down. My yearly receipts do not represent so much income actually received, for, as has been stated previously, there did not appear to be a market for garden produce in Flushing, but are given as the amount I should have had to pay if I had bought the various articles at retail prices. This is clearly proper; for, if we had wanted them to eat, had purchased them at the stalls, and had paid the current charges, there would have been just so much additional outlay; that we did not eat them is no answer, for we could have done so had we wished.

This exhibit was certainly entirely satisfactory; the account had steadily improved, and bade fair soon to show a large income. I have even gone so far as to leave out of question rent saved, dissipation at Saratoga avoided, health improved, digestion invigorated, pure air enjoyed, and a thousand other matters for which we pay so dearly; I merely take the hard, dry figures—the positive profit and loss in dollars and cents—and they give a clear net profit of nearly eight hundred dollars. Nothing could be asked more promising than this; if it went on improving at this rate, there was no telling where it would stop. Farming had evidently proved itself a source of vast wealth. We were nowhere near the limit of the productiveness of my five acres, and, with additional attention, we might reasonably anticipate increased returns. The result was so encouraging, the life at

Flushing so charming, the access to the city so easy, that I resolved to move there permanently. There was much to be done besides sleigh-riding and skating, even in the winter months; roots had to be stored from frost, bulbs required attention, potatoes and turnips demanded care, chicken-coops had to be built, forcing-frames dug, and a green-house erected. Taking all these things into consideration, I resolved to abandon the city, and, in spite of frozen ground, deep snows, piercing winds, and muddy roads, to devote myself to agricultural pursuits.

CHAPTER XVIII.

PREPARATIONS FOR REMOVAL.

IN the last chapter I have stated that so charming did the country seem to me, so pure its pleasures, and profitable its cultivation, that I resolved to remove there permanently, and give up entirely the less lucrative, if more distinguished, pursuit of the law. A most essential preparation for this change was the necessity of cultivating and increasing the present stock of plants—the tender and fragile things requiring winter protection—which the abundance of the last year had left me. My stock was not, perhaps, what finished gardeners would call choice; they were not those out-of-the-way foreign productions which only rejoice in one name, and that a polysyllabic Latin one; but, although they were equally entitled to a scientific appellation, they were generally known under common ones. I had an abundance of carnations, which I had sometimes referred to as varieties of *Dianthus caryophyllus* when my uneducated city visitors called to see me. There was quite a stock of scarlet geranium; for, although I had ordered from the florist at Flushing a dozen different colors, he had determined that one kind would answer my purposes. There were a few of the exquisite *bellis perennis Hortensis*, more generally known as daisies. But of all my treasures, the most numerous of any one kind was a great variety of verbenas, which I had raised from seed, and which had sported into every variety of color, except —as Weeville once said when he was in an envious mood—a handsome one; but tastes differ.

These valuable plants must be protected during the winter, and preparations had to be made to insure their being turned into the beds the ensuing spring in healthy condition. To this end it was necessary to add to the books of reference. To "Breck's Book of Flowers," and Rand's "Work on the Garden," which I already possessed, I added Beust's "Flower Garden Directory;" Leuchar's "How to Build Hot-houses;" Todd's "Young Farmer's Manual;" Fuller's "Small Fruit Culturist;" Warder's "American Pomology;" Dr. Chase's "Recipes, or Information for Every Body;" Mead's "American Grape Culture," besides a number of others equally learned and abstruse, in addition to subscribing for the *American Agriculturist*, I put my name down for the *Farmer's Friend*, and the *American Farm-*

er, as well as the London *Field*, which always contained a valuable article on "Work for the Week," that gave me a number of important suggestions. The thorough study of these for the space of a month made me perfectly acquainted with the subject in hand; they not only told me all about green-houses and window-culture, but gave me valuable hints about propagating vines, pruning trees, increasing and improving manure, building concrete walls, skinning sheep, sawing logs, chopping down trees, and concerning a vast number of other subjects, all of which information might prove exceedingly useful some day or other if my farming enterprises proceeded.

By the aid of these works it was ascertained that plants could be grown advantageously in a room of an ordinary dwelling-house, provided the proper care was exercised. This was quite satisfactory, as, unfortunately, I had no other place than the fourth-story room of my house in the city to devote to my new protégés. Under the published directions, which I studied over till I had them by heart, a room with a southerly exposure was selected, a staging was erected in front of the windows, and the gas was so secured that no thoughtless person could turn it on and poison the air of the extemporized green-house.

The preparatory study and the final execution of the plans recommended had somewhat delayed the fall potting of the plants, until a few frosts had warned me that there was no time to lose. Unfortunately, when I appointed a day for effecting the transfer from the garden to pots and boxes, and went to Flushing for the express purpose, I discovered, to my dismay, that Patrick was in a great state of confusion as to which flowers were hardy and which required removal. As my reading had not extended to that question, or I had forgotten it amid the extensive list generally catalogued, I had to go mainly on what might be called general principles. By general principles is meant that, as the cold had been pretty severe, it might be presumed to have exercised a preliminary influence on the tender species; so, wherever a perennial was observed to be withered and have a sickly appearance in its leaves, it was taken up and potted.

Fortunately, I was well acquainted with the characteristics of verbenas, carnations, and Johnny-jump-ups, and selected them without trouble; but as to other matters, I felt, to the last, that there was considerable uncertainty. The verbenas having struck root at every joint, and as I felt that not one must be lost, a very considerable number of pots was necessary, and the time I could spare for personal supervision was exhausted long before the work of transplanting was accomplished. It was necessary, therefore, to leave Patrick to his own unaided resources, with such advice and instruction as it was probable he would appreciate.

He evinced his usual enthusiasm and self-reliance, and within a few days arrived at my city residence with a wagon full of what the books termed "bedding plants," and assured me he "had the likes of that three times over." The labor of carrying a hundred pots full of earth up four flights of stairs is excessive; and ere Patrick's reserve was exhausted, I was much the same myself. Nevertheless, perseverance conquered, and we finally transported the last pot, managing to break less than a dozen on the way. Unfortunately, some of Patrick's trips were made during a cold snap that we had, and it is possible that the frost slightly damaged the plants, which did not seem exactly healthy when they arrived. There were some among them that I did not recognize accurately, and one in particular looked so strange, that I inquired of Patrick what it was. In answer to my question, he scratched his head for a second, poked his finger under the stunted foliage, peered in among the leaves inquiringly, and finally said au-

thoritatively, "That! why that's a verbayny, sure; and yer honor knows a verbayny as well as meself." "But, Patrick, that does not look at all like a verbena; it has a very different leaf. Are you confident that you are right?" My honest servitor looked at me a moment reproachfully, and then replied interrogatively, "And does yer honor think I'd be after decaiving you about such a thing as a verbayny?" Of course, there was nothing more to be said, and the difference in leaf, which seemed so puzzling, must have been due to what florists would designate as a sportive change in the plant—possibly the first specimen of a new and valuable seedling.

I tended those plants carefully; water was given them regularly, the windows were opened on every genial day, and the directions contained in my books were marked, and re-read daily, to insure the observance of every important point. Still the plants did not seem to thrive. They grew weaker slowly, but steadily; every morning found them less vigorous, and often was marked by a premature death. In fact, the living ones diminished quite rapidly, and ere a month had elapsed nearly all had perished utterly. This epidemic was peculiarly fatal among my verbenas, although the books had described them as being rather unusually hardy; and with the exception of Patrick's new seedling, which was vigorous enough, they were either dead or dying. This was quite an appalling state of affairs. Recourse was had to my literary counselors; recipes were found for curing mildew, bugs, borers, red spiders, and a large number of other difficulties, but nothing on the subject of general debility.

My flowers had no active disease, unless it were an analogy to human consumption, or what our quack doctors describe as a loss of manly vigor; and as these complaints are not referred to in horticultural works, and as the medicines guaranteed to cure the human frame could hardly be expected to benefit them, I scarcely knew what to do. In despair, I purchased some whale-oil soap, and proceeded to wash the leaves with that highly-recommended compound. Perhaps whale-oil soap is not advantageous in general debility; perhaps it was made too strong, or applied too often. Under its application, my future progenitors of bedding beauties perished faster than ever. A solitary fuchsia, that had been purchased the spring previous, went early; the roses followed precipitately; the daisies were not far behind; the verbenas made haste after these; the carnations followed in this headlong race, until, in spite of the most tender care, the most scientific nursing, the most approved protection and artistic cultivation, ere spring arrived, the entire collection was dead save one—that famous new seedling verbena of Patrick's discovery. It still lived, not flourishingly nor enthusiastically—not as though it could endure much more assistance—but, as the pleasant days were near at hand, exhibiting sufficient strength to last till the winds of heaven could be trusted not to visit its cheek too roughly.

My assiduity in tending that solitary plant was praiseworthy. Nothing was left undone that could insure its welfare; water, warmed to a proper temperature, a sufficiency of fresh air, occasional supplies of a little new earth or well-rotted manure, a gentle stirring of the surface, and pruning of straggling and superfluous sprouts—none of these were omitted. In spite of this attention, it remained pale, yellow, and feeble, so deadly must have been the nature of the unknown and invisible malaria that had penetrated into my green-house; but it survived the danger. It became gradually weaker as March passed by and April advanced, but was still alive when, in May, after it had been carefully hardened off by progressive exposure to the air, it was once more consigned to the earth of the garden. The fuchsia was gone; the roses, the daisies, the carnations, were no more; its brothers had fallen by the way-side; but this peculiar variety—this child of my own raising—this new species, that had no equal for hardness, and probably would have none in beauty—this seedling, that was destined to electrify the floral world—this original discovery, which I had already mentally resolved should make my name immortal as the *Verbena Barnwellii*—was saved! That was all-sufficient.

Weeville had inquired from time to time how the scientific cooking-shop, as he ironically designated my green-house—because the dry furnace-air which ascended to the upper story did make it rather warm—was progressing, and sarcastically remarked that a hundred new and healthy plants could be bought in the spring for what it would cost to keep one over the winter. But I had too much confidence in the books which I had studied to believe in his old fogy notions. I had put him off with "glittering generalities," intending to keep my discovery a secret, and enjoying by anticipation his amazement and rage when he should find that a mere tyro, by scientific appliances, could surpass an experienced hand like himself, and do that which was beyond his utmost hope—originate a new variety. I had intended waiting till my plant had recovered its vigor under the influence of the "wanton wind" and the warm sun; but as it did not improve rapidly, and no doubt missed my fostering care, I took an early opportunity to invite him into my garden.

There were a number of roses, fuchsias, and other bedding plants that I had just purchased and set out, and he remarked at once, with a laugh,

"So your cook-house did not work; you have had to buy new plants after all. Furnace-houses, with dry, hot, parched air, are poor places for green leaves and thirsty vegetable mouths. Moisture is a necessity to the cultivation of flowers, and it will not answer perfectly when applied only to the roots."

During this discourse I had led him toward the new seedling, and at the proper moment I replied,

"That may be true; but the satisfaction of tending one's own flowers is great; the pleasure of watching them is sufficient reward; and then there is always a chance of effecting something original."

"Yes, there is that, no doubt. Amateur greenhouses are original enough."

"I mean there is a possibility of making some discovery, of starting a new variety. For instance," I said, slowly and impressively, "look at that; is not that reward enough for all my trouble?"

"Look at what?" he replied, peering about in a stupid way, striving not to notice the wonderful plant at his feet, and stopping in a doubtful way when his eyes finally rested on it.

"Ay, look at it. Study it well," I continued, enthusiastically. "Examine its texture and its foliage; observe the delicate edge of each leaf; the tender strength of each spray. Conceive its future freshness of beauty, and the glory its discovery will confer."

"Are you talking of that?" Weeville inquired, giving the sacred flower a sacrilegious shove with the toe of his boot. "Why, what do you take that for?"

"What do I take it for? You may well inquire. I take it for the *Verbena Barnwellii*, the crowning glory—"

"Verbena fiddlesticks! It is nothing but a weed—a piece of wild sorrel, just like a dozen others hereabouts, for they seem to abound in your garden—only it is rather miserable looking, and is near about dead from some cause or other. But what has that to do with your city green-house?"

Explanations were unnecessary. Patrick had made a mistake; he had either taken up a weed for a verbena, or had potted a weed and verbena together, and the verbena had died early, for certain it was that my new seedling, the puzzling variety of an old species, was nothing but an ugly specimen of worthless sorrel. It died soon after. I was glad it did. Possibly scientific hot-house culture is not beneficial to weeds, but until it perished of itself I had not the heart to dig it up, and thus put a violent end to so many vain hopes and promising anticipations. The *Verbena Barnwellii* is still in the undiscovered future. Patrick had committed other errors; most of the plants that he had taken up ought to have been left out, and most of those that were left out should have been taken up. The results of this practice convinced me that Weeville was right, and that it is cheaper to buy plants than to raise them, even with all the aids of modern science; and that, if any gentleman finds too many weeds in his garden, he has only to remove them to his green-house and cultivate them assiduously to exterminate them rapidly.

M

CHAPTER XIX.

A GREAT RUNNER.

IN describing the unfortunate termination of my efforts to winter our stock, I have advanced a little beyond the regular order of events. There was much other work to be done in the garden, even without referring to the masses of bedding plants and the quantities of new seeds that I had purchased. As the third season opened, a renewed energy took possession of me, and I went at digging and planting like a giant refreshed. There was no longer a sense of desolation around my place. The florists and nurserymen, under my careful instruction, had set out trees, and planted flowers, and got hedges in order, until Nature in my five acres was bursting from a smile into a grin. It is true that the cows of the neighborhood, which were invariably allowed to roam whithersoever they listed, had fed rather profusely on the evergreens, breaking down the tops and nipping off the ends of the branches; that here and there the hedges had died out, and left yawning gaps; but, on the whole, there was a remarkable change. It was at this point that I bethought me of an omission from my flower garden which was as surprising as it was inexcusable; hitherto I had neglected doing justice to the gourd tribe.

I am great on gourds; they are my specialty. I will undertake to grow them against the world, and will meet Jonah in a fair field, and no miracles, any time; in fact, I am a perfect Jonah on gourds. In early youth, when my gardening was confined to a city yard, my gourds were the first, and fattest, and yellowest to be seen; and, from that remote period to the time of which I speak, I had always felt an affection for the beautiful fruit, and wondered why Nature did not put more in it. Of course there must be gourds in my garden, in spite of their being a useless production and very hollow—Weeville made a joke about their beating other fruit all hollow— and, except to make fragile water-dippers (which, by the way, no one ever makes of them), quite worthless; so I not only planted the seeds in the open garden, but forced some in the hot-beds.

My special favorites were three seeds of an almost unknown variety, called Hercules' Club, upon the past history and future prospects of which I could get little information. I planted these little germs of promise in a prominent place in the front beds, and watched with tender care till they came up. A pale, delicate, juicy little spear, guarded by its two seed-lobes, pushed its way above ground, where it seemed ill suited to battle with the breeze and brave the sun, that threatened to break or consume it. My solicitude became greater when the feeble stem put forth a feebler leaf, not larger than one's finger-nail, and so thin that the tracing of the veins was like gossamer. My horror, therefore, can be imagined when I found, on the ensuing morning, that a squash-bug had fallen upon my tender nursling and eaten the leaf all up.

I killed that bug. He endeavored to slip into the earth, but I slew him without remorse. He was not an ugly bug in outward appearance; entomologists might even have called him handsome; his colors were a mixture of gilt and black, but his beauty was no protection. The next day another delicate leaf rewarded my protection, but the following morning another squash-bug devoured it; he met the fate of his predecessor; but, when a third leaf was disposed of in the same way, the result began to be doubtful; the question was arising, which would give out first, the squash-bugs or the leaves? Having heard that wood-ashes was good to drive away bugs, I was about applying a dose, when Patrick assured me that they would "scorch such a little mite of a thing all up;" and, as I had already discovered that no reliance could be placed on tobacco, I was nearly at what ladies call their "wits' end"—whichever end that may be, when Weeville again came to the rescue.

"Squash-bugs!" he said; "there is no need of ever being troubled by them. Nature always has a remedy for all Nature's ills, if we only look for it. Onions, my boy, are the thing. Does a squash-bug ever eat an onion? No, sir. Then make him eat it, and see how it agrees with him. I used to be bothered with them among my cucumber-vines till I put a few onions in each hill. No more bugs now. I never lose a leaf—not a single leaf. When you plant gourds next time, put in a few onion-seeds at the same time, and you will have no trouble. The smell does it."

This was very fine for the future, but I wanted to save my Hercules' Club for the present; so I thought to myself that if onions would answer when grown in the vicinity, why would they not answer if removed to the place, and kept renewed from time to time? There was no scarcity of onions, and if we did not use them in this way, it was doubtful whether they would be used at all, so I immediately gathered a quantity, and built a breastwork of bulbs and stalks round my little pets. At this time the sprouts were bare, having been stripped by our remorseless enemies; but next morning still another leaf put forward its claim to recognition — somewhat weaker, perhaps, than the earlier ones, but still a leaf. By sundown it was fully developed, and my anxiety can be imagined to learn its fate next day. I was up and dressed by sunrise, and, to my great delight, found the leaf there and no squash-bug.

The victory was won. The fatal *chevaux-de-frise* was renewed daily, and proved itself an effectual barrier to the foe. One leaf followed another; they increased in size; the stalk mounted a few inches, and was secured to a stake. This appeared to be the turning-point of the plant's existence. It suddenly began to grow, and, having exhibited its feebleness in infancy, now commenced to show its strength. In one night it grew a foot, and up it rushed, in a few days, to the top of the stake. There were three plants in all, not far apart, and they had soon climbed as high as they could on their supports. Huge broad leaves, as large as a straw hat, made their appearance. Fresh stakes had to be inserted, and then, when these were covered, which happened in a few days, still larger ones were substituted. My skill had been tested in inducing the wonderful plant to grow, and I was not to be outdone now. Hoops were arranged from post to post like a single section of an arbor; cross-pieces were added, and still the plant outran them. I was becoming weak, and, having beaten Jonah, was trying a match with Jack of the famous "Beanstalk," with heavy odds in my own opinion that I should win. It was still early summer, and where my gourds would end ere the season was over seemed doubtful.

Unfortunately, at this stage of the contest there came up a storm of wind and rain. This was a contingency that had not entered my mind. My supports were frail, my lashings insecure; in an instant the whole structure was leveled to the ground. Without waiting to tear my garments, as I should have done if I had been Jonah, I rushed bareheaded into the storm, fearing that an hour's delay would give the gourd a start never to be overcome, and again raised my frame-work and secured it more firmly. Still the gourd grew. I led strings in all directions, but, not satisfied with these, it spread over the ground, covered my small plants, crawled up the neighboring bushes and trees, crept out into the paths, and threatened to occupy the entire garden. I was still bravely contending against the inevitable, when destruction in the shape of another storm came upon me in the night, and the following morning found my labors again stretched upon the ground.

This proved too much for me, and, giving in at once, I called Patrick to do what he could under the circumstances. He straightway sunk two stout posts and braced them with guys in every direction, and then we let the Clubs—of which these certainly seemed to be the kings—follow their own fancy and grow till they should be tired. Being in a conspicuous part of the garden—in fact, pretty thoroughly hiding the smaller flowers—our friends had been deeply interested, and, never having seen the vine before, wondered what kind of fruit it bore. It had produced abundance of white flowers, in shape somewhat like the yellow blossoms of the squash, but they fell off, "leaving not a wrack behind," nor any fruit. I could not find that Jonah's gourd, or the beanstalk of my friend Jack, had produced fruit or left seed, and began to think that mine was an exceptional production of a similar character, that could only be raised by those who were great on gourds, or, as the Vulgate hath it, "some pumpkins." If Jack's stalk had produced beans, we should have known those beans; if Jonah's gourd had borne seed, we should have found them at the seed-stores to this day.

My anxiety was greatly relieved, therefore, when at last something that was evidently intended for fruit made its appearance. It was almost of the size and shape of a small lead-pencil, and closely resembled a long green worm. This remarkable fruit—only odder, if any thing, than the parent that bore it—after the same hesitancy and dilatoriness, commenced to grow in the same mad way. It was soon as thick as your finger, then as your wrist, then as your arm, and considerably longer than the latter; and, ere it gave up, became as large round and longer than a small man's leg. Hercules, even, would have been bothered to manage such a club.

It bore seeds, but I destroyed them. My squashes were ahead of all in Flushing. My pumpkins ran for hundreds of feet, climbed the bean-poles, and bore a large fruit on top, one specimen being huge enough to have furnished Peter Piper's wife with a comfortable apartment. My ordinary round gourds attained the size of a child's head; and if I produced such a result as I have described from my first year's attempt with the Hercules' Club, I was not prepared to take the consequences of a second or third effort.

It was better to allow such a plant to disappear; the discovery of new species of flowers and vegetables is creditable so long as they are either handsome or useful, but to get the reputation of being the man who originated a wonderful gourd, to go down to posterity celebrated for this alone, to be spoken of in horticultural works as the gourd-man, was too terrible a fate. Moreover, there was some danger in renewing such an experiment; on the second trial the wonderful plant might have spread all over the neighborhood, climbed upon crops, strangled trees, surmounted houses, and invaded the village in such a way as to make me liable for damages for trespass. There are some things which a man does too well to do often; growing gourds was evidently one of those with me, and I determined never to be led into such an undertaking again.

To counterbalance this wonderful success, it is necessary to record a remarkable failure. "Variety is the spice of life." It is this variety which gives agricultural pursuits their principal zest; no two attempts in planting bring about the same results. There may be the same circumstances of time, place, and weather, but the conclusion will be altogether dissimilar. All honest farmers must confess—and farmers are, like lawyers, without exception, upright and truthful—that the return from no two years has been alike. One year the potatoes fail, another leaves us without corn, a third is too much for the wheat; then the fruit rots, or the turnips will not grow, or the sweet potatoes run entirely to vine, or the oats to straw. Something never comes out right, or does what was expected of it, and often behaves in a shabby manner. Of course, my horticulture could be no exception, but the eccentricities of Flushing soil are rather extravagant, although the editor of the *Agriculturist* lives in the neighborhood, and does all he can to keep it in order. I have mentioned some peculiarities of my hot-house experience. I will give certain facts, quite as strange, relative to out-of-door gardening.

There were some hardy perennials which I had raised with great care, and among them a fine specimen of crimson flax, or what I had satisfied myself was crimson flax. My seeds had fallen into a little ·confusion in consequence of the names getting washed off the labels by the rains; but, as the plant bore a crimson flower, and did not resemble any thing else in particular, I had made up my mind it was crimson flax; if it were not, there must have been a defect in Thorburn's seeds, which is not to be presumed, for nothing else of that description came up. Perennials are not generally satisfactory during their first season; they make a poor growth of it, showing a feebleness that is extremely painful to a fond and devoted gardener. They are not easily distinguished from weeds at best, and, as they grow far slower than the latter, are often lost entirely among them. For this reason I was especially proud of my crimson flax. It grew thriftily, spread into a good-sized bush, and covered itself with delicate flowers.

This had occurred during the previous season, and when fall came I was careful to mark the spot where it was with several large stakes, in order to warn Patrick against digging it up. Patrick was rather an enthusiast with a spade, and somewhat zealous in weeding; he was fond of digging up the garden to "mellorate" it, as he expressed the idea, and to prepare it for spring planting; and if he had not the flowers very distinctly and plainly marked, he would, in the excitement of the operation, dig them up ruthlessly. So also, in weeding, he had to be warned and watched, for more than once was my blood frozen with horror at beholding Patrick weeding up a valuable plant, and twice he weeded all the young sprouts off a flowering shrub so effectually that the shrub never recovered from the shock. With this fear before my eyes, and a question about the perfect reliability of my own memory, I marked the spot where my crimson flax was located with great care, surrounding it on all sides with stakes plainly lettered. Thus fortified, I waited confidently till the winter should be over, having put my own weaknesses and Patrick's at defiance.

True to my confident expectations, with the first few warm suns my crimson flax reappeared amid its palisade of stakes. It grew far more strongly than before, spreading rapidly into a large bush, and requiring the assistance of supports and strings to keep it in shape. There was an odd singularity about it, however, which struck me as remarkable. The leaf seemed different from what it had been before—it was longer and narrower; but this probably was one of those changes which perennials undergo ere they get firmly established, and, among the many curious things I had experienced, did not surprise me particularly. The plant was on the exact place where it had been the year previous; it was growing luxuriantly, and bid fair to be a magnificent ornament to the garden, for it had a prominent situation. I did not boast of it, however. Boasting is not natural to me. I did not even call Weeville's attention to it. He had disappointed me so often that I resolved he should be disappointed himself. I was determined to say nothing until it should be covered with its crimson gems.

It grew remarkably. If it had done well the previous year, it bid fair to surpass itself this season. As its time for flowering approached I became quite nervous and excited. Slowly the buds formed, being almost innumerable, and covering each spray; they filled and distended, and finally burst. But what was my astonishment when I discovered that they had changed their color. Instead of the rich crimson flowers that were expected, I found the bush one morning covered with strange-looking blossoms of a dull yellow. The most remarkable transformation ever known had taken place—crimson flax had lost its natural hue under careful cultivation, and assumed the appearance of a cross between an orange blossom and a dandelion; if any thing, it was rather more like the dandelion. It was no longer crimson —had, in fact, no shade of crimson. It was a pure yellow, and not altogether a handsome one. To describe the disgust that this unexpected change wrought in my usually placid temper is impossible. I began to hate that plant. The more it blossomed the more furious I felt, until finally, when it had covered itself with these wretched straw-colored abortions, my feelings overcame me, and I pulled it up by the roots.

This burst of passion has caused me much regret.

By a moment's indulgence of anger I destroyed the chance of raising a new species of plant, a changeable crimson flax—crimson one year and yellow the next. Weeville, when subsequently informed of my indiscretion, attempted to console me by endeavoring to make out that it was a weed which had smothered the original flower. He even doubted whether there ever had been any crimson flax in my garden, and pretended dissatisfaction with my description of that plant. He said he was not aware that crimson flax was a perennial, and thought that the designation in the catalogue was an error, ridiculous as such a supposition was to my mind. He undertook to show me numerous weeds by the road-side — for weeds are quite abundant in Flushing—which bore yellow blossoms, and which he felt confident were the same as the one I had raised. They did resemble it in many points; but, as I had marked my plant carefully, had seen it blossom the year previous, and knew whereof I spoke, I utterly disdained his explanation. I must still feel that the loss of my new flax was serious, and must regret the outburst that led to it. Even a flower convertible into a weed, or changing biennially from one to the other, would be rare and curious.

Moreover, although we did raise several garden

weeds, this was like none of them. They were most deceptive things, and imitated the appearance of plants wonderfully. One grew quite tall, and seemed to be on the point of flowering all the while, but never did so. Another spread into quite a large tuft, something between a daisy and a violet, and imposed upon Patrick, even, so thoroughly that he never dug it up in a single instance, notwithstanding his readiness to extirpate whatever was of doubtful authenticity. It spread rapidly, until it was quite a labor to pull it up. Another of these troublesome members of the vegetable kingdom attained almost the dimensions of a shrub, and had a thick, solid stalk, and actually flowered; but the blossoms were the minutest things possible, and bore a ludicrous disproportion with the size of the bush; while the snapdragon obtained a hold in the beds which it is probable I never shall eradicate, by an error of appreciation continued through a few months. In fact, the weeds performed such strange antics, and behaved in so unexpected a way, that the question arose in my mind as to what was a weed. The author of "Ten Acres Enough" says that it is a flower out of place. The latter half of his explanation may be well enough; but as to its being a flower, most of those that came up in my garden had no flowers whatever. Without entering too far upon a religious disquisition, it may do merely to suggest that it struck me that weeds were original sin, springing up to trouble us every where, and calling for that sweat of the brow which is ordained as the lot of the human kind for the first great crime of Mother Eve.

The nature of weeds is exceedingly perverse. They seem to have been sent to torment man, sprouting up continually without apparently ever becoming exhausted, causing an immense deal of unnecessary annoyance. As an evidence of their innate perversity, it is only necessary to refer to the manner in which they behaved toward my *portulaca splendens*. This showy plant had been thriving admirably, and as its seeds, when allowed to sow themselves, naturally reappear in augmented splendor the following year, I had founded great expectations upon the anticipated result. It is true that the portulaca did sow itself, and did come up finely the present spring; but, unfortunately, weeds come up without any sowing. They originate or "come of themselves," as my brother farmers lucidly express it, and they appeared with the portulaca, and grew twice as rapidly.

The end of it was, that, although the flower was there, and even matured, it was hidden so effectually that there was no way of getting a sight at a blossom except by pulling up a yard square of weeds. My conclusion from this—and valuable it is to the cause of agriculture—was that our scientific men had not paid sufficient attention to weeds; that they had taught us how to make things grow, but had not told us how to prevent their growing; that an anti-fertilizer was more important than a fertilizer. There is twice as much labor expended in rooting weeds out as in putting vegetables in. We have our phosphates and superphosphates, our guano, marl, bone-dust, lime, and a dozen other species of manures, but not a single invention to prevent undesirable growth. The present necessity is a drug or acid, or some sort of medicament, that will kill all the weeds and the germs of weeds in the ground, but which will soon lose its power, so that the ground will perform its proper functions when seed is planted. Until this discovery is made, farming will be laborious, and I hope our learned men will devote their attention to it promptly. I shall only claim the honor of originating the idea, and leave the entire profits to the inventor.

CHAPTER XX.

A BEAUTIFUL NEW COACH.

I HAVE already mentioned the honesty of the people in Flushing. Nothing is more pleasant and satisfactory than to deal with persons on whom one can rely; to feel that one gets precisely what is agreed upon—can trust entirely to the word of the seller. To be sure, they were now and then a little too confiding. They had a way of supplying any person in the village with whatever he wanted, and charging it to me. If I objected, they answered conclusively that he had given my name, and that they were not accustomed, in the country, to doubt every man's word who applied to them for a keg of nails or a dozen boards; and they explained that confidence was the foundation of business. Rather than disturb this creditable, almost too creditable state of affairs, I submitted, and paid for a good many articles that went to other people. I made a short attempt to enforce a rule that any applicant who gave my name must have a written order, and I even opened a pass-book with the leading store-keeper; but these innovations met with so much opposition, and the leading store-keeper had always so much to add to what appeared in the pass-book, that I gave up the effort, and accepted country ways of dealing.

Even the farmers were affected by this simplicity of views; they had peculiar and somewhat unwise opinions, but they held to them religiously. They believed in New York as the Moslem believes in Mecca; they considered that they must make all their sales there, and that weekly pilgrimages thither were a necessity of their success in life. No inducement would persuade them to sell any of their produce on the road, or short of that sacred destination. It was vain to apply to them for a load of hay, or a dozen bags of oats; they would cart these six miles over heavy roads rather than sell them within a few rods of their doors. This was inconvenient, but a sure guaranty for their honesty; none but very honest people could be so simple, and their faith in the metropolis of the nation was actually touching.

"Sure, yer honor," said Patrick to me one morning, "and the new Rockaway is gone intirely."

"Why, Patrick, you surprise me; I only bought it last spring." I did not say that I had obtained it second-hand, as it is well not to forget appearances, and human nature is somehow or other ashamed of buying any thing second-hand. The fact was that Dandy Jim had pretty much used up my first wagon; he had run away with it so often, had dragged it over so many fences, and smashed it so frequently and so effectually, that, when he was sold and the new family horse was purchased, a new wagon had to be bought for him. I said nothing to Patrick about its being second-hand, and he said nothing to me; we neither of us pretended to be aware of a fact which both of us knew perfectly well. True to his instinctive Irish delicacy, not a word was breathed against the honor of the house to which his fortunes were attached. So he replied,

"Be gorra! and it was a beautiful wagon intirely when yer honor brought it home; you may well say that."

"What is the trouble, then, now?"

"Sorrow a one o' me knows, but they tell its going fast, and I thought it was me duty to spake about it before any accident happened, which would be a pity, indade, indade."

"Is there any thing wrong with the axle-trees?" I inquired, anxiously, worried at the implied risk.

"Axle-trees! whirra, and they're as strong and

sound as the day they were put in; divil a word can be said against the axle-trees."

"Well, then, is it the springs?"

"The springs! Now did yer honor ever see a purtier pair of springs in yer life?"

"Perhaps it's the wheels?"

"The wheels! divil a bit is there any thing the matter with the wheels; better running wheels, when they're well grased, were never put in a wagon at all, at all."

"Then, Patrick," I cried in despair, "what on earth is the matter?"

"And didn't I say it was wake all over, it was; and if it comes down when yer honor's out driving, you mustn't blame me. Yer honor knows best, but I shouldn't like to be in it if it did break down; but perhaps there'd be no harm done—you may be going slow, like, and the horse may stop."

"Patrick," I responded, still more appalled at this picture, and not at all confident of so fortunate a result, my experience having been rather the reverse— "Patrick, it will never do to run any risk. What shall I do about it?"

"Yer honor does not seem to care for it, but, as I tould yer honor before, there's a beautiful new coach down at the carriage-maker's. If you saw it once, you would be much plased; it's lovely intirely. If you would only get that, that would be the doin' ov it."

This discussion was not altogether an unusual thing between us. My Rockaway had been growing weaker and weaker for some time past, and, as its weakness became more striking, the "beautiful new coach" loomed up more distinctly. At first the spring would want strengthening, then the axles would need examining, next the tires would require resetting, and so on, until an application to the wheelwright became an event of weekly recurrence. On each repetition, the attractions of the "beautiful new coach" would come under discussion, and be dilated upon, although, as I had little faith in country work, and entire confidence in my Rockaway, I turned a deaf ear to all such suggestions.

However, matters had been becoming more serious lately. The wagon had certainly acquired a wobbly motion, which was neither agreeable nor reassuring. The springs or wheels, or both, appeared to have lost their strength; the latter did not track quite true, and, in turning a corner or crossing a gutter, there was evidence of a defect somewhere. No special difficulty had made itself apparent, but there was a general giving out — a sort of grogginess all over.

The whole concern "yawed about" and "slewed round," as the nautical gentlemen express it, after an unpleasant and threatening fashion. It was apparent that something must be done, and the carriage-maker, who also had the "beautiful new coach" for sale, declared that repairing would do no more good; so to Patrick's last remark I responded with resignation,

"I suppose I shall have to get a new wagon of some sort. What does the man ask for the one you speak of?"

"Only three hundred and fifty dollars, with pole and shafts. Mr. Jones paid him four hundred for one just like it last week, but he says he wants yer honor to give him a chance. There's nothing but the best of stuff gone into it. He puts on new patent clips; and the painting is the loveliest blue and red that iver was seen."

"Well, Patrick, you may drive me down, and I will look at it."

"Thank yer honor; and shall I hitch up right away?"

"Yes; the sooner it's over the better."

"Thrue for you, and so it is; for a break-down would be a pity, with the doctors charging so high. But ye'll be safe enough in the new coach."

We found the wheelwright at his shop, and ready to expatiate on the many good points of his vehicles and the excellence of his work; the advantages he had over city builders, and the danger there was in riding in a broken-down affair which was made of such wretched stuff as mine, that he only wondered had held together as long as it had. The proposed carriage was quite gorgeous and very fine with paint and upholstery. I thought it rather heavy for one horse, but Patrick, who had taken much interest in the discussion, immediately, on my making the suggestion, seized the shafts, and ran it up and down as if it were as light as a feather. So there was nothing for it but to say that I would take the "beautiful new coach;" and, stepping to one side with the maker, I said, "I am informed that the price is three hundred and fifty dollars."

"Oh," he replied, "that is without the pole; with the pole it is three hundred and seventy-five. Mr. Jones paid me—"

"Never mind about Mr. Jones. I understood the price was three hundred and fifty dollars with pole and shafts; but, as I do not want the former, I will do without that."

"But they both go together," replied the man. "Now I'll tell you what," he added, dropping his voice to a confidential whisper, "you have been a good customer of mine, and I want to please you; so let's say three hundred and sixty-five, and that will be almost throwing the pole in. It costs a good twenty-five dollars to build one."

I never liked haggling over trifles, so I consented and paid down the money. I did not send for the new carriage immediately; in fact, a change seemed to have come over the Rockaway; it gave up wobbling, the wheels ran steadier, the springs became stronger, and its general debility disappeared. It was altogether a changed vehicle. I heard no more complaints from Patrick, and all danger in using it seemed to have disappeared, for he took five of his female acquaintances to church in it the very next Sunday morning. When we did get the new coach home it proved to be entirely too heavy, and Patrick was the loudest in declaring it was "no good at all, at all." Of course, it could not have been that an honest village wheelwright would purposely have put my wagon out of order that he might sell me a new one, but such a sudden recovery of health on the part of a Rockaway was extraordinary and wonderful to the last degree.

Of course, when a man moves permanently into the country, he builds an addition to his house. Why

he does so, neither he nor any one else can tell. He
never does the like in town; no additional room is
necessary, but he does it all the same. I was attacked with the same mania, of course. The only
way of adding to my house was by putting a second
story on the main wing; there was no possible mode
of extending either side, or erecting an adjoining
building, or doing any thing whatever except moving a step nearer the heavens. This implied the removal of the roof. Now a roof is a very necessary
thing; people who have been in the habit of living
under one know little of the inconveniences of doing
without it, even for a short time. It is ornamental—
may have a pretty border, or edging, as our farmers
say; but it is not only ornamental, it is extremely
useful; and if any reader doubts this, let him remove
the roof from his house, and try the effect of a
change. The foundation is necessary, the sides are
advantageous, but the roof is essential.

As fate would have it, my alterations were commenced in March, which is not altogether the best
month for such things, in view of the fact, little ap-
preciated by citizens, that that month is the commencement of the rainy season. So the tin was
rolled up and taken off, the rafters were pulled
down, the sides of the additional story were com-

pleted—and then it rained. I had prepared as well as I could to meet this contingency, being the possessor of a large amount of canvas, which once constituted the racing sails of a yacht that I owned in my younger days, and I had spread this over the yawning gulf as well as I could. But it did not answer; perhaps there was not peak enough, or the duck was worn thin by age; certain it was that it leaked, and leaked badly, not in mere drops, but in rivulets, that first covered the upper floor, and then worked their way down through the lower ceilings, and dripped on the furniture, and discolored the walls, and loosened the plaster.

Moreover, the rain always came at the worst times and in the most disagreeable ways. I would go calmly to bed, leaving every thing apparently serene, not a cloud in the sky, the stars shining brightly, and the wind due west, and be waked up at midnight by the beating of the storm, and the trickle of the water as it came down through one corner, its favorite spot, in my room. Then the wind would blow, and work under the canvas, and tug at the ends, until it succeeded in rolling it up, so that it could expose what was beneath.

And then, of course, at the precise moment when a dozen more days' work would have made me safe

—when the windows only were wanting, or a few more boards would have shut out the destructive element—the carpenters and sash-makers concluded they would enjoy a little "strike"—preferring leisure to work, and needing a short rest from their labors. Many a time would I be roused from my comfortable bed, and be forced, with quite a scanty amount of clothing, to climb up the rickety, half-finished stairs at midnight, and get drenched through putting up boards or nailing down the canvas; for water,

useful as it undoubtedly is for some purposes, can do so extensive and unexpected an amount of damage; it gets into such odd places, and produces such queer results. However, Patrick, true to his Irish nature, was so delighted with my example that he determined to follow it, and begged time enough to build himself a house. When my troubles were about over, I met him one day, and asked how his building was getting on?

"Thank yer honor," he replied, joyfully, "I am doing finely; there was a frind, begorra, and true frind he was, and a carpenter at that, and he has built it all for nothing, because he was out of work. Sure and it's an ilegant house."

"Well, then, Patrick, I suppose you'll soon be moving into it."

"I would that, but for wan thing."

"And what is that?" I inquired.

"It hasn't any roof on it."

"You don't say so; why, that is quite important."

"Thrue for you, yer honor, it is that; the flure and the sides is beautiful; it has two flures and a roof as purty as ever was."

"Why, I thought you said it had no roof," I responded, growing somewhat confused, as I often did over Patrick's explanations.

"Oh no; the roof is all there, but it lakes, it does."

"Still, if it does leak, the upper floor would catch that, and you might occupy the lower story, as I have been doing."

"So I would, indade, but the flures have no boards on them; nothing at all, at all, but jest the bare bames. But I wouldn't mind that meself, and me family would do well enough on the ground if it wasn't for the lakes, and the bad saison it is at that."

"You ought to find out where the leaks are, and stop them," I replied.

"Sure, and it lakes all over."

"Now, Patrick," I remonstrated, "how can it do that? No roof was ever made that leaked all over; the thing can't be."

"Well, yer honor knows best; but when a roof hasn't any shingles on, it lakes purty bad."

"Patrick," I said, pausing and looking at him sternly, "what on earth do you mean by saying one minute that you have a roof, and the next that you have none?"

"Well, yer honor knows the boards for the roof is all there, and put up beautiful, but I hadn't any shingles, more's the pity, and me paying rint all the time, and me frind with nothing to do until he gets some work, and no telling the day when he may do that. And I thought perhaps yer honor will give me the loan of some shingles, and keep the house yerself until I could work it out. The windies ain't much matter, and boards will do very well, but sure a house is good for nothing intirely unless it has a roof on it."

I coincided fully in Patrick's views; there was a bond of brotherhood in suffering between us; and although I did not keep his house for him, he had his shingles. And so he was fairly housed, and my extra story being completed, and the garden having at last consented to grow, and the trees to furnish foliage and give yearly promise of fruit, and my vast experience having been carefully stored away for the use of others, and myself finally and peremptorily settled in the country, I think it is time that I closed this veracious and trustworthy account of "Five Acres more than Enough."

CHAPTER XXI.

THREE HUNDRED ACRES NOT ENOUGH.

I AM writing this supplementary chapter after the expiration of nearly fifteen years since the record of my farming experiences was commenced; and while I have nothing to take from the interesting statements which have been set forth in the previous pages, I have much to add to them. Everything has gone on as it began, with the same invariable pleasure, profit, and satisfaction. The field and the fields of my labor have alike been one long delight—from the soft yellow of the upturned surfaces when the plough had just prepared them for the seeds, through their period of emerald-green promise and their crowning glories of fruitful russet and gold, till they passed under the snow-white mantle of their wintry death. My success on "five acres" was so triumphant that I purchased a farm of twenty-five at Rockville Centre, and subsequently one of two hundred at Sayville, and to those have kept perpetually adding till they number three hundred and fifty, and bid fair never to be enough. My feet have trodden all the highways and by-ways of successful agriculture, and my efforts have done much to solve the great problem that the world has been groping over for four thousand years; for only when science shall teach just how much hydrogen, nitrogen, superphosphate, hydrocephalus, tredecem radiatus, esox reticulatus, and cerebro-spinal meningitis make up the component parts of every stalk of corn, grain of wheat, or head of oats will the human race be redeemed from darkness and ignorance, and all men made rich and happy.

Patrick and I built hot-beds and cold-frames; and if the hot-beds did come out cold-frames, and the cold-frames occasionally endeavored to be hot-beds by burning up all the plants in them, we were sure to get one or the other almost every time. Moreover, we have had our triumphs as great as those of war. We have raised the mammoth squash, a miniature planet of orange loveliness, bursting with beauty and solid with succulence—so roomy, that Cinderella would have found no trouble in using it for her coach, or Peter Piper for a wife-protector. It was sent to the county fair, where it was much admired by my friends, and caused much envy in the mind of Weeville, to judge from the disparaging remarks he indulged about the taste and value of squashes. It would have taken the prize were it not that another farmer had sent one a few pounds heavier, although far inferior in contour and general excellence of expression. Ours should have had a second prize, but that the chief official informed me that they never gave second prizes for squashes.

Of course there have been drawbacks, but what mattered it if the commonplaces did not come up to expectation, if the turnips and carrots failed and the grass dried up. Who could not spare the horse vegetables in the land of the pea, the Lima-bean, the asparagus?—where there was never too much heat or drought for the sweet corn, and where the luxuriant egg-plants would spread out their broad green hands to the generous sun in gratitude for his rays in summer, and would round out their purple globes in the cool days of September and October—that is, when the potato-bug did not eat them all up. Insects have become rather overabundant. Indeed this might be said to be the bug age, in contrast with the stone age and the iron age and the golden age which have passed before. There is every known and unknown sort of insect on Long Island. The Colorado beetle paid his respects promptly, on his evolution, and has remained permanently; the borers bore our apple-trees; the curculio swarms in our plum-trees; moths and army-worms and tent-caterpillars and every other sort of creeping and stinging thing assist our labors and share our profits.

The poor broken-backed farmer has fallen upon the day of small things — the winged, creeping, crawling, and ever-devouring small things of six legs and more or less wings and unlimited stomach; those that delve in the ground and worm their way into roots, or climb up the branches and eat the leaves, or which strike the fruit and spot and blight it. He must poison the potato-beetle, he must burn the galleys and cities of the tent-builders, he must prod the borers with wires. By comparison with these the hum of the ever-present mosquito is but a humbug, and his bites flea-bites.

Following the directions of enthusiastic bug sportsmen I tried to inveigle the innocent moths into the candle of destruction. Patrick was directed to place a lamp in the orchard and set it in a pan of water with kerosene oil on the surface. There was every reason to expect that the moths from their known weakness for light would have rushed to this death-trap by myriads. But Patrick soon gave the most discouraging accounts of bug behavior and insect artifice.

"Arrah that was no good at all at all," he said in a disgusted tone. "They wouldn't be after going widin a mile of it."

"But, Patrick," I replied reprovingly, for I was afraid he had not given the experiment a fair trial, "they must have been within a mile of it, as the orchard is not a quarter of a mile either way, and they seem to be as plenty there as ever."

"And your honor may well say that. Plenty, is it? There is no end of them, and they keep growing on us every day."

That was a personal way of stating the case which made my flesh creep, and sent itching sensations over my whole body. So I asked him hastily,

"Then why did you not try the lamp?"

"Try? And sure and I did that same. Och, but it burned beautifully, and all the country round could have seen their way to steal our fruit, only there wasn't any fruit to steal. More's the pity."

"Well, what did you catch?" I asked impatiently.

"Catch, is it? Sure the first night I caught a mosquito and a house-fly, and the next night I caught only a mosquito. I didn't think it worth while to be wasting oil at that rate, for we would be a hundred years before we caught all the bugs in our orchard; and then, more be token, they would grow ten times as fast."

Since the commencement of my horticultural operations I had had on my mind and in my heart a longing for a bed of mushrooms. The realization of this dream had been postponed in consequence of a certain obscurity in the directions contained in my authorities. Bridgeman was very enthusiastic and hopeful, but slightly incomprehensible. He said that the bed must be established in "a light cellar." Now none of my houses had a light cellar—neither the first one imported from Nantucket, which might be expected to produce any imaginable eccentricity, nor that old-fashioned farm-house at Rockville Centre, nor the modern production of lath and plaster. It is true that when the first was in the formative state—had got as far as the cellar and no farther—in which condition it remained, as has been explained, that part of the construction was as light as could be wished; still I felt in my soul that the necessary cellar must be the cellar of a house, not a house that was all cellar. If Bridgeman had only said a light garret, I could have accommodated him. But all cellars I had ever entered were dark. Or if there had been some way of putting a cellar out of doors. I could have introduced the gas into the cellar, but was afraid to burn it or kerosene lest they might burn too much. I was all in the dark about the cellar, and doubted whether artificial aid if attainable would convert its inherent darkness into the light of Bridgeman's intelligence.

He said if there was no light cellar we might use an old shed. But here, again, was a similar difficulty. We had no old shed; they were all new: besides, they were not much lighter than the cellar. Light was evidently necessary, and it was only after much thought that I hit upon a feasible plan. We had built a sort of greenhouse; it had not been used long, the plants not proving green enough to live in it, and it had been converted into a chicken-coop for the forcing of infant chickens. No better place could be selected, if light was wanted; for the sun poured down upon its glass roof and sides all day long, till the chickens got so over-heated under the forcing process that they spent most of their time, when they were not engaged pulling out each other's feathers, standing and panting with their mouths open. Here it was that I determined to establish the mushroom-bed, where it would have a sure chance to heat, and where it could have as much light as the lightest cellar Bridgeman had ever discovered.

When I subsequently mentioned my intentions to Patrick, he made incoherent remarks about "its being too hot intirely, and that the sun would burn them all up." But he had not studied the habits of mushrooms and their demand for light; so we picked out "the droppings," as we were ordered from day to day, and turned and flattened them, and laid layers of earth between layers of them, in the most approved manner. The middle of August arrived before we were through, and the place was so hot I fairly gasped as I worked in it; but when it was completed, I broke the cakes of mushroom spawn into pieces, and deposited them under a few inches of soil, and covering the whole with a deep mass of straw, awaited developments. It was some time before any results made their appearance; then there was a motion in the earth, which, at first I supposed was the activity of the seeds and the bursting forth of the fruitful fungi. Nothing of that sort came of it. Instead, the motion extended itself till it resembled a gentle movement of the entire bed. At this my suspicions were aroused, and I proceeded quietly and cautiously to investigate. I lifted off the straw from one corner, and stirred the earth and dug down into it; then the truth came upon me. There was a motion—a motion through the entire conglomeration of earth and droppings; but it was not of the bursting fungi, nor even vegetable in its origin; it was entirely vermicular: the bed was one wriggling, moving, turning, twisting mass of worms. They might have been a new development of the worm family—a sort of mushroom worm produced by spontaneous generation; but I had not the heart to investigate them, under the knowledge that all our efforts to produce a bed of mushrooms were to end in the production of a crop of worms.

I said nothing to Patrick, but carried out the straw, and let in the chickens once more. They had got a fresh growth of feathers from running about the grounds, and had accumulated a healthy appetite, and the way they scratched and dug and dusted in that mushroom-bed showed the extent of our misdirected results, and assured me that if we ever wanted to raise chickens all we had to do was to establish a mushroom-bed on the most approved principles, and in a light and sunny exposure.

Hardly, however, had the painful admission of our failure been forced upon us, when a special Providence, as it might be called, or an agricultural equipoise, came to our assistance. I had laid out a portion of the garden for a plot of fall spinach, and told Patrick to give it what is politely termed a "good dressing"—a ball costume, or regular wedding outfit of manure. This had been planted, but gave no signs of coming to fruition; at least Patrick assured me that he had "put lashings of seeds into it," although doubts began to arise whether he had not forgotten that important step in successful agriculture. The plants certainly did not show up, although we were now passing well into the autumn, and I was wondering how I could turn that "dressing" to account. One morning, as I was studying the problem, I noticed that there had been a movement in the soil, such as I had at first hoped from my mushroom-bed. Little mounds had erected themselves here and there, as though the tiniest of gnomes were at work, or the spinach had collected itself in spots for one tremendous and united effort to break through the stubborn soil. I instantly suspected more worms, and thought of turning the chickens from the hothouse into the garden, but before doing so resolved to investigate.

To my equal surprise and delight I found, on uncovering one of these mounds, that they were the mud-homes of the precious fungi, and that the mushrooms which were vainly sought in the light of science, were the mound-builders, and had surreptitiously transferred themselves to the garden. There are many surprises in horticulture, and especially in mushroom propagation. Having produced a bed of vermicular life when I was in pursuit of fungi, a reward of fungi had equalized matters by usurping the place of a plot of spinach. I watched those succulent eccentricities with the attention they merited. I lifted the earth off their tender heads lest they should be pressed back into the ground. I gloated over their creamy consistency, so superior to the dull discoloration of the vapid and faded objects purchased in the markets. At last my well-earned triumph was to come, and Weeville was to be taught that, although I might not succeed precisely as I had planned, intelligence and study were sure to be crowned in the end. The weather was growing cooler, the season being early, and I felt that no time was to be lost.

I proceeded promptly to make a collection of the luscious edibles as soon as they were sufficiently matured and abundant, determined to use them as a surprise to my friends in the city, including Weeville, who was not to escape from my triumph now. There was no depending on the uncertain future, for the grounds of glory were in the basket. I telegraphed an invitation to a supper at the Manhattan Club, merely saying I would bring a dish from my farm that I thought would astonish my friends, and teach them that there was something in home-farming after all. It was a big basket and well filled, that there might be no stint, and weighed so heavily when packed that I put it on the piazza out of the sun till Patrick should bring up the horse. The horse was rather restive; horses always are restive till you get in, and seem to be in a terrible hurry, and there is no end to their anxiety to be under way till they are, when they generally become more moderate. Our horse was peculiarly unsteady on this occasion, and Patrick had all he could do to control him as I climbed over the wheels, for years of hard toil in the field have made me stiff in my limbs, and slow in climbing. So we started in some confusion and trepidation. It was only when the train had reached Jamaica that I found that I had forgotten all about my basket of mushrooms, and had left it calmly resting in the shadiest part of the piazza.

The little party went off very pleasantly at the club, and I left the guests mystified as to which special dish it was that had come from the farm, although Weeville in his blunt fashion blurted out that he believed " I had made another failure of it."

That night there came a severe frost, and not only were all the mushrooms that had been picked shrivelled up, but those in the garden were killed. I kept that spot sacred next season, hoping that the treasure of the earth would again present itself: but the little genii never favored me thereafter; nothing but weeds grew the ensuing summer, and after that we converted it to the raising of corn and cucumbers. This was a disappointment, but I had the satisfaction of feeling that I had raised the finest mushrooms that ever were seen, and could raise them again, provided they took into their heads to appear as unexpectedly as in this remarkable instance. It is a permanent pleasure to dwell on the thought of how good they would have been, if only we had had a chance to try them, and had not forgotten that basket, and I never can pass that portion of the garden without a reawakening of such sentiments, and if any visitors happen to be with me taking occasion to point out to them my mushroom-bed.

www.ingramcontent.com/pod-product-compliance
Lightning Source LLC
Chambersburg PA
CBHW022052230426
43672CB00008B/1146